Highlar̶
Country Diaries

To Zandra

with best wishes

from

Ray Collier.

First published in

The **Guardian**

Highland
Country Diaries

Ray Collier

Illustrated by
Iain Serjeant

Colin Baxter Photography, Grantown-on-Spey, Scotland

To ValC because...

First published in Great Britain in 1997 by
Colin Baxter Photography
Grantown-on-Spey
Moray PH26 3NA
Scotland

Text © Ray Collier 1997
Illustrations © Iain Serjeant 1997

ISBN 1-900455-28-5

Printed in Great Britain

Cover Picture © John Love 1997

Contents

1	Achvaneran	17	Loch Flemington
2	Amat	18	Loch Garten
3	Ariundle*	19	Lochindorb
4	Badentarbat	20	Loch Maree*
5	Beinn Eighe*	21	Mallaig
6	Berriedale	22	Monach Isles*
7	Dirrie Moor	23	Nairn
8	Dunnet Links	24	North Rona*
9	Fort William	25	Oldshorebeg
10	Glen Strathfarrar*	26	South Uist
11	Inchnadamph*	27	Spey Bay
12	Inverpolly*	28	St Kilda*
13	Isle of Mull	29	Strathdearn
14	Isle of Rum*	30	Strath Fleet*
15	John o'Groats	31	Struie
16	Loch Bran	32	Tarbatness

* National Nature Reserves

Acknowledgements

Appreciation of the Highlands and its wildlife can be a solitary experience, whether looking for small blue butterflies on the banks of the River Findhorn, standing in the middle of a rookery of grey seals on North Rona or looking for selkies at Sandwood Bay. Many times, however, that appreciation has been enhanced by the company of like minds – they will know who they are – who have shared this enthusiasm, especially the old-style wardens of reserves and I thank them all. I am also indebted to the Letters Editors of *The Guardian* and the patience and support of the Publisher and his staff.

Foreword

At midday the two otters were playing in a sea loch off the island of Mull, and in a way those two animals were responsible for starting my Country Diaries in *The Guardian*. It was in 1987 and I had previously sent two Diaries in but was told that the newspaper had their own regular Diarists, but that if I did one about Mull the editor would be tempted. A few months later I became one of the regular Diarists in place of the late Ted Ellis, the famous Norfolk naturalist.

The Highlands and Islands contain a wide variety of habitats and a rich and often spectacular wildlife and the chance to explore them over 27 years has left numerous indelible impressions in my mind. Most of that time was as Chief Warden for the Nature Conservancy Council responsible for the management of 28 National Nature Reserves in the north-west, a region that covers an area one million acres larger than Wales!

To many people this landscape and its wildness is epitomised by the red deer stag, red grouse, salmon or golden eagle but there is much more that stirs feelings and imagination. The deep purple flower of the Scottish primrose on the north coast, the clamour of the gannetry on St Kilda, the tiny chequered skipper butterflies near Fort William and the huge grey seal rookery on the Monach Isles. These are wildlife spectacles, sometimes involving comparatively rare species, but there are many other more subtle delights: the scent of a swarm of fragrant orchids near Inverness, the courtship flight of Scotch argus butterflies on roadside verges, dimples on the water made by brown trout rising in a hill loch, the porcelain look of cowrie shells at John o'Groats, or miniature dragon-like great crested newts in an old curling pond. The aim of these Country Diaries is to share these experiences and adventures with readers in the hope that it will enable them to have greater enjoyment of the wildness of the Highlands and Islands.

Living in a strath just south of Inverness – together with five miniature dachshunds, a springer spaniel, two African pygmy goats and numerous poultry – has given me an insight into the rural scene. Otters, badgers, curlew and mandarin ducks all breed close to our old farmhouse where there is a variety of habitats. However, in other parts of the Highlands there is cause for concern as large tracts of the landscape have been degraded, and still are, by over-burning, over-grazing by sheep and deer and over-intensification of other farming techniques. We may be planting trees and giving small parcels of land some 'protection', but until these basic issues of degradation are dealt with we are, in real terms, only marking time.

We cannot live without wildlife and wildness
Whether its form is to be our sanctuary of thought
Or to set a stage within which we ourselves are known.
Woodland, wetland, mountains and moorland are essential
To our own lives and wildlife has its own right to exist.
If we fail to conserve this heritage we fail ourselves,
Fail those who are yet to come, and fail wildlife.
The responsibility is ours alone, each and every one,
To take stock and ensure the future – without compromise.
And so to arms and each in their own way to take a stand
Thus joining the battle to preserve the wildness and life.

Ray Collier, August 1997

Pine Marten

Winter

At Lochaline we stared southwards across the water to Mull while we waited patiently for the ferry to appear round the headland. In the sea loch were red-breasted mergansers, black guillemots and eiders whilst over the far shore a buzzard was hunting – no doubt for rabbits. But despite the wildlife our thoughts strayed back to earlier this century and the famous evacuation of St Kilda in 1930. For it was at Lochaline that the St Kildans were brought ashore, many of them to work in the Forestry Commission that is still clothing the landscape with conifers. Long before that, however, this ferry route had been important for cattle and our ferry took us to the same point on Mull where the cattle would have landed – Fishnish. From there we followed the old droving road west to Salen on the south side of the Sound of Mull.

The village is now comparatively quiet compared with the days of the cattle market, or tryst, where cattle were sold before droving them east and then south on the mainland. Mull was the gathering point for this part of Argyll, including cattle from the rich grazings of Coll and Tiree. Throughout the main droving period of the eighteenth and early nineteenth centuries up to 2000 cattle a year crossed from the east point of Mull at Grass Point to the mainland coast near Oban. The gathering of cattle from the neighbouring islands as well as from places on Mull itself such as Tobermory, Oskamull and Calgary, meant that there was a whole system of rough roads and tracks through the mountains of Argyllshire. But such routes were already present as the traditional byways for kings, nobles, churchmen and pilgrims to gravitate towards Mull and then Iona. For Iona was the spiritual centre of Scotland and beyond and the burial place of the Scottish kings.

This is a sea loch between the islands of Ulva and Mull and we were driving along the very narrow road – with passing places – on the north side of the loch. It was from this road that we saw the otters which at first, without looking through binoculars, were two dark shapes diving and reappearing amidst the ripple across the loch. Then binoculars revealed a pair of otters that were feeding and, as far as I am concerned, playing. Some of the time they were swimming on the surface close together then suddenly they would both undulate on the surface, disappearing for a few seconds as though looking for fish. Then a more positive move as one, closely followed by the other, would arch upwards and then down into a dive that left the tail poised in the air for a split second before each disappeared for a long time.

It was from one of these dives that one of the otters surfaced with a crab about 4 in (10 cm) across the back and immediately both otters turned to the shore and, on the surface, swam towards us, landing on the boulder-strewn water's edge about 30 yds (27 m) opposite our vantage point, affording superb views of their antics. During the swim the presumed male lunged once at the female who shook her head and carried on, ignoring the threat. When they landed, however, the male showed no interest in the food whatsoever and whilst the female tackled the crab he simply foraged amidst the seaweed nearby.

The female seemed to take a long time to demolish the crab – about ten minutes or so – and when she had finished the two otters joined up again and started foraging along the shoreline, moving steadily along the loch. Then for no apparent reason they slipped into the water almost without a ripple. Then the same hunt and play pattern until they were too far away to be seen comfortably – a memorable sighting at midday.

Whilst looking at some specimens in the storage rooms of the Inverness Museum and Art Gallery I was shown a box containing three mounted moles. As it was a museum you could perhaps expect to find such things, but not a black mole, a white mole and a piebald mole. The white fur on two of the specimens was slightly creamy but I guessed this was fading with age and originally they had possibly been an albino and a partial albino. Unfortunately there was no information as regards date or origin and later I could find no reference to colour variety in any of my books. Fortunately the museum kindly lent me the three specimens and on my monthly field trip with BBC Radio Highland I mentioned the moles at the end. I asked for any information on them and also whether anyone had seen any colour variations because in my own 40 years of being interested in wildlife the only moles I had ever seen were black. With enquiries being directed to the museum, we were delighted with the response as a few people telephoned and a small number visited the museum to give information. One person said he thought the moles had been caught by a mole catcher on the Ness Castle Estate in 1926. Other people said they had occasionally seen white moles in other areas so the three moles from the Museum had obviously created some interest.

Two weeks later someone called into the museum with a golden yellow mole found at Ness Castle Estate and on close examination it had white fur tipped with golden yellow. For me it was back to the books again and at last I did find a reference in *A Vertebrate Fauna of the Moray Basin* by Harvie-Brown and Buckley published in 1895. They had a few records of not only white specimens but also grey and a form with 'pale yellow bellies'. Most records were from the Inverness area but they had one albino from Sutherland. It seems therefore that colour variations in the mole are a lot commoner than I for one had believed.

The drive along the north coastline of Caithness and Sutherland – from Scrabster to Durness – gave us tantalising views of the sea and occasional cliffs where fulmars and gulls were riding the light breeze. Between these views, however, the bleak moorland was frosted white and most lochs and lochans were frozen over with not a single bird or mammal in sight. The distant hills of Ben Hope, Foinaven and Arkle looked even bleaker as they formed a backcloth of continuous snow over the high tops. In contrast, just west of Durness, the bay at Balnakeil was a hive of activity with small groups of birds or individuals scattered over the sea. The yodelling calls of the displaying long-tailed ducks could well have been likened to children calling from the sand dunes as it is such an unlikely bird sound. The nearest trio of long-tailed ducks, two drakes and a duck, were so noisy that they soon attracted the attention of others as there were eventually 16 of them displaying. Drakes would rush over the surface of the water calling loudly and then, as if at a given signal, all the birds would suddenly dive and stay under for a long time. As they

Whooper Swan

14

were so close to the shore even binoculars could pick out the attractive pink and black banded bill and the white ring round the eye.

Further out there were three single great northern divers feeding steadily, along with a single red-throated diver and a scattering of shags. A male and two female goldeneye were about the same business but in contrast the loose flock of about 50 fulmars were just resting on the water with only a few of them preening. But there were also fulmars on the low cliffs and yet more skimming over the cliff top only to plane down to the water and zoom up again, making it look so easy and scarcely flapping a wing. Far out on the water the telescope revealed a black guillemot in its black plumage with white side patches and at one stage it turned over in the water and there was the sudden flash of bright red legs. The breeding plumage was a little surprising as only the day before we had seen two black guillemots at John o'Groats in the whitish plumage of winter.

As if this was not enough there was plenty to see around the freshwater loch behind the dunes. As we walked over the dunes a flock of snow buntings circled us several times and on one flight they were joined by two pure-looking rock doves. The loch had coot, tufted duck, red-breasted merganser and two whoopers and whilst looking at the swans we realised we had seen four small herds of whoopers that weekend totalling 18 in all, but all adults – a poor breeding season somewhere!

There is no such island as St Kilda as the name refers to the archipelago of islands 50 miles (80 km) west of the Western Isles that includes the islands of Hirta, Soay, Dun, Boreray and Levenish. Hirta is the main island and a February day this year found me sitting on brown and green cushions of thrift on a high ridge overlooking Village Bay and, to my right, the village itself. My eyes were constantly drawn to the grey shells of the old houses in wonderment that people lived in this harsh and element-torn island. Even the Soay sheep seemed to add to the sense of awe as they fed amidst the many walls and cleitean – turf-topped stone structures used by the St Kildans to store various items. At this time of the year most of the sea birds have left the island although thousands of fulmars were still on the cliff faces. A few adult gannets drifted past and two black guillemots were in the bay, whilst a solitary raven croaking overhead added to the various sounds that penetrated the constant background noise of the sea crashing through the narrow gap between Hirta and Dun. To my right a group of Soay sheep were grazing the very short turf overlying the long ridges of runrig that swept down to the cliff edge. Directly in front of me lay the jagged outline of Dun and even at this time of the year numerous breeding holes of puffins were easily seen. In the summer Dun carries some of the densest colonies of puffins – part of the 300,000 pairs of these 'sea parrots' supported in this archipelago.

But there is another interest at this time of year, as around October the grey seals haul out to pup and through binoculars I counted 15 adults and 11 large pups still on the rocks. Then, lost in imaginings about the St Kildans, I ended up at the burial ground and some of their harsh life could have been summed up by the inscription on the headstone of a 20-year-old man who died in January 1898: 'With Christ which is far better'.

At the first thin layer of snow we drove up the hill over the opposite side of the strath from our house and we were soon up to the highest point at 1400 ft (427 m) and looking over a very bleak landscape that we had not ventured into before. At first there seemed very little to see but slowly we picked up the various signs of wildlife and then started to see species. In the snow were many tracks of mountain hares – we were too high in this area, and in the wrong sort of habitat, for them to be brown hare. Tracks of red deer criss-crossed the road in many places on the way up but it took the binoculars and then the telescope to find them. They were there in their hundreds with large groups of hinds and smaller groups of stags and quite separate, although with the hinds, there was the usual sprinkling of young stags, called staggies.

Red grouse called and then eventually a male and female appeared on the ridge behind us momentarily silhouetted against a snow-threatening sky as they flew rapidly over and dropped quickly to the river below. It was obvious that we were in grouse moor country because of the patterns of muirburn areas scattered all over the landscape. How good to see a mosaic of small areas of muirburn where the grouse could feed on young shoots and then rapidly seek shelter from avian predators in taller heather close by. A crow and a hooded crow flew silently past as if respecting the silence that dominated the whole scene whilst a buzzard way down below us by the river sat hunched up on a boulder the whole time we were there.

We were to see two other birds of prey, however, as on a drive further down the glen we had a tantalising view of a golden eagle, and then a kestrel flew up from the roadside as if it had dropped on to some prey. But meanwhile the grouse had started up again until a raven croaked overhead and the silence returned as if by order. That silence of the Highlands is one of its attractions at any time.

One feature of my work in conservation is the increasing number of questionnaires that land on my desk, whether it be information on the facilities for disabled people on reserves in the Highlands to people who ask for so much information they could write a book on what they request. However a recent questionnaire started me thinking, as it was on the species of freshwater fish that occur on the 28 National Nature Reserves in the Highlands. As an angler myself, I mentally started ticking off those species that came to mind and the list came to five: salmon, brown trout, stickleback, arctic char and eel.

At the end of the exercise and thanks to the wardens in the Highlands, the list amounted to no fewer than 15, although to be realistic this included four species that admittedly were found in fresh water but only because rivers ran through brackish conditions and into the sea. These four species were flounder, saithe, sand goby and three-lipped mullet. One surprise was that arctic char only occurred on two reserves but the species needs deep water and deep lochs on such sites are not common. In contrast it was also surprising to find that the brook lamprey, with its eel-like slimy shape, was found on six reserves. This fish has no mouth as such but sucks blood from live fish. Its relative the river lamprey, sometimes called the lampern, normally migrates to the sea in late summer to spend its adult years in the sea but returns to spawn in the spring and dies. Not surprisingly, therefore, it only occurred on one reserve, namely Mound Alderwoods on the east coast of Sutherland. As one might expect, the brown trout was the most widespread species with records from 22 reserves, which is even more significant considering the fact that four of the sites are not suitable for trout. The second commonest was the eel at 20 reserves and it even occurs on St Kilda some 50 miles west of the Western Isles. The other species were pike, sea trout, two species of stickleback and minnow.

A male great spotted woodpecker has been a regular visitor this winter to our garden bird table. Early in March we also heard the call notes and drumming from the birch trees further up Strathnairn. On a day in the middle of March 'the' woodpecker came briefly to the table and a call from the kitchen informed me that my wife considered it was a different bird – a female. We had pondered often as to the whereabouts of a female, if indeed there was one around. As this bird had been in view for mere seconds my response no doubt indicated my scepticism but five minutes later the bird was back again and the absence of red feathers on the nape proved it was a female. I will not relate my wife's comments but suffice to say it will be a long time before they are forgotten. As if this was not enough, later that morning a Sea King helicopter coming low up the strath put up a golden eagle that soared over the woodland only to be joined by two others. There was no display, just effortless soaring as they went up and up before drifting out of sight.

In the afternoon we walked to the River Nairn a field away from our garden and there on a sandy bankside were the perfect sets of tracks of an otter. Then in the long narrow ditch running back to the garden we found fresh clumps of frogs' spawn from about 15 females. It was here too that we found a dead heron not many yards away from where, earlier in the winter, a dipper had succumbed and we realised that with luck we could get herons visiting our planned garden pond in the paddock. We ended the day planting cuttings of pussy willow against the bottom fence – 44 in all – whilst brief flurries of snow reminded us that winter could still have a few tricks up its sleeve in these northern parts. During that day there were ten siskins and ten greenfinches at the bird table but at the other end of the garden the wild bluebells could not be denied as their leaves were over 1 in (2.5 cm) out of the ground despite settling snow.

My original introduction to the works of the botanist G. Claridge Druce was not from his plant recording but rather from his references to the Northamptonshire poet John Clare. Clare, at the beginning of the nineteenth century, used to be a shepherd on heathland to the west of Peterborough and the area coincided with the National Nature Reserve I wardened in the 1960s. Druce, in the foreword to his *Flora of Northamptonshire* published in 1930, devotes 25 pages to Clare, a man who after his death was called 'The finest poet of Britain's minor naturalists and the finest naturalist of all Britain's major poets'. Druce recalls seeing Clare outside the asylum in Northampton and his research on Clare's plant records indicates that he mentions no fewer than 135 species of plants in his poems, of which 40 were 'first records' for Northamptonshire. Druce's flora became a botanical Bible for me.

Then in 1969 I moved to become warden of Inverpolly National Nature Reserve in Wester Ross. One of the first moves I made was to find out if by any chance a flora had been written for the area – most unlikely I thought at the time, as in those days it was considered to be a remote area and to a certain extent still has this reputation. Then I found out that a flora had indeed been written and by none other than G. Claridge Druce and, typical of his floras, the introduction was fascinating! In August 1881 he first went to what he describes as 'a land of mountain and of flood' and found that 'means of communication were then so bad I had to carry a knapsack, a vasculum and a small drying press with me'. He had difficulty in recording on the hills of Beinn Eighe as the shooting tenants refused access but Druce sauntered up the Torridon road in mist and rain sporting an umbrella and raincoat as if for a constitutional. He then jumped under a bridge and followed the watercourse out of sight of the keepers.

Within minutes of leaving Inverness airport I was looking down on the snow-covered high plateau of Ben Wyvis as the plane went north-west to Stornoway. The next high plateau was Ben Dearg which was also covered by extensive snow fields in contrast to the Summer Isles just west of Ullapool. The islands were the brown of winter heather with here and there small areas of green of the first spring bite of grass. It was easy to see just how sheltered is the bay on the east side of Tanera Mor as the rest of the islands' coast was being hit by sea water that sent large areas of spray over the rocks as it was whipped off the tops of the high waves. The island furthest west in the attractive archipelago is Priest Island of Fraser Darling fame and it seemed almost covered with spray as we headed further west. The immediate visual impact of Stornoway is not the town itself or the extensive peat banks and cuttings or indeed the harbour and ships. It is in fact the large areas of woodland in the grounds of the castle that contrast so sharply with the otherwise bleak moorland.

Then it was into the Twin Otter aircraft for the short trip to Benbecula with the comment from the pilot that we would be at only 500 ft (152 m) to get below the weather – I can only remember ever travelling at 500 ft (152 m) on this trip! The fields of Benbecula are a patchwork of green along the west coast and as always I had to force myself to reach my destination of Loch Druidibeg National Nature Reserve. Distractions – if that is the right word – were the pairs of lapwings displaying in territory, as were oystercatchers, redshank and mute swan, although as if to put the season in context there were still flocks of lapwings and golden plover. Standing in the warden's empty house at the reserve and speaking to the incoming warden, we saw a hen harrier that drifted across the loch towards the house and hovered 10 yds (9 m) away from the window and but 3 ft (1 m) off the ground.

On Good Friday we sat in the car in a strath a few miles south of Inverness while the rain and snow showers swept up between the snow-covered hills. By the river, swollen with meltwater, 26 oyster-catchers were feeding – perhaps the breeding population for the whole of the strath – and when occasionally they flew up and round, the pure white of their under-feathers matched the white of the snowy backcloth. Suddenly about 30 red grouse flew up from the hillside and on reaching a good height flew off into yet another snow storm and then we saw the reason for this sudden behaviour. An immature golden eagle drifted across the hillside with the white rump and white patches on the wings clearly visible through binoculars. The eagle seemed intent on something, as a few flaps of its large wings took it purposefully out of sight and it ignored the occasional single grouse that took off in a flurry of wings.

We had stopped near a scree slope where a single mountain hare, still in its white winter coat, sat motionless whilst around it a small group of wild goats were eating lichens from some of the larger rocks. This tribe have their kids much later than any other wild goats we know in the Highlands, as all the others had theirs in January. There were three kids in front of us, two being less than a week old and the other probably only two or three days. The two older kids were pure white but the other one was an attractive mixture of brown and silver although its nanny was pure white. Then our attention focused on four brown hares that were chasing each other and we had the unusual experience of seeing both mountain and brown hares at the same time. It was one of those days when everything went just right as we counted eight groups of goats with 48 nannies and ten kids with still more to come. Then there were the red deer stags and hinds, the former still with antlers whilst at the east end of the strath a group of eight sika deer hinds grazed near the woodland.

Loch Ruthven   *14 January 1990*

Although there was flooding in a number of places, remnants of snow piled up along roadsides and some lochs and lochans still frozen, we ventured out to Loch Ruthven about 10 miles (16 km) from home. We drove past Brin Rock – a series of cliff faces that I wished still had wild goats amidst the steep rocky slopes, birch and larch trees but they were shot out in the late 1950s. There is a fine dark head of a billy in the hall of nearby Aberarder House, which was one of the last to be shot on Brin Rock. The lochan below the rock lies next to the inn appropriately named the Grouse and Trout. There was a female or immature goldeneye diving after food, indicating that many lochs were still frozen as it was the first time we had seen this species on this lochan. Part of Loch Ruthven is a comparatively recent reserve which is owned by the RSPB and there is a well-prepared track leading to a comfortable hide set amidst the birch woodland that fringes the north-east corner of the loch. As expected there were no cars in the small car park but at least the track was clear of snow and we were soon shuffling through the mud that melted snow and rain had produced.

Last time we had been at Loch Ruthven the calls of common sandpipers, common gulls and Slavonian grebes had filled the air but now there was that silence of the Highland winter that in itself was captivating. There were signs of wildlife, however, as there were droppings of a pine marten in the middle of the narrow track we were following and on the sandy strip at the edge of the loch there were clear impressions of where a roe deer had walked. The log book in the hide indicated that the last visitor – the day before – had seen nothing but had commented on the ice to the right of the hide, which was now piled up over a large area by the wind from the south. We began to think that we would see no birds, but the telescope revealed some mallard in the water under the alders on the far shoreline.

As we had called our existing dachshunds after islands on National Nature Reserves – they ended up as Kilda, Rona and Sula – we were determined to follow this tradition when our two new puppies arrived. As with the other three they are both miniature long-haired dachshunds and their naming was a source of great discussion. One of the puppies is a normal black and tan but the other is the much rarer silver dappled that has only recently been 'accepted' as a colour form of the breed. To start with we looked at the various islands in the St Kilda archipelago again but although some of the names are attractive, such as Boreray, Dun, Stac Lee and Stac an Armin, none seemed to fit. Soay seemed a suitable name but for some reason it is sometimes difficult to pronounce and after much discussion we excluded it from the list of possibilities. We then turned to another archipelago about 50 miles (80 km) to the east of St Kilda – the Monach Isles near the Uists. The earliest name for this archipelago is Heisker and it is still its official name today, although on the Admiralty Chart it was changed to Monach Isles to avoid confusion with a small island to the north called Haskeir. So one of the puppies is called Heisker but that still left the silver dappled one. As it happened this was not difficult: although one of the islands was formerly known as the Monach Isle in the late seventeenth century because there was a monastery there its true name is Shillay and so the other puppy became Shillay.

Heisker's first sighting of snow was a good 8 in (20 cm) deep outside the back door at the end of December. She leapt into it and disappeared apart from the very erect tail that protruded a few inches above the snow line. Shillay was a close second followed by the three older dogs and the snow flew everywhere as tunnels were formed under shrubs; together they formed a network of U-shaped depressions all over the garden as they bounded around, obviously enjoying themselves with their tails all fully erect. When they came in the two puppies had blobs of snow on their noses but little elsewhere, while in contrast Kilda, with his long black and tan hair, was a mass of snow balls. There were plenty underneath him and on his bib there was a compact lump of snow a good 3 in (8 cm) across; as he stood in front of the Rayburn for me to clear them off he looked positively proud of them.

Kilda the
Dachshund

The first frogs' spawn in the area this year appeared on the Black Isle on the night of 19 February – two weeks later than last year but almost the same date as in 1988. It prompted me to visit our 'favourite' pond at Essich about 2 miles (3 km) south of Inverness, a pond we have regularly looked at for over ten years. The pond is on the side of a narrow road over open moorland and most people would pass it by without a second glance as it is only a few yards across and in the centre about 3 ft (1 m) deep. In spring the lapwings and curlew breed nearby and later in the year white flowers of grass of parnassus are dotted over the damp sides of a tiny burn that flows within yards of the pond. For such a small area of water the pond supports a wide variety of wildlife and over the years we have often dipped with a pond net and still find it thrilling to peer into the net once it has been dragged through the pondweeds.

Judging by the number of clumps of frogs' spawn each spring there is a healthy colony of frogs there and with so many mild winters in recent years most of the frogs have stayed in the water all winter. Some frogs spend the winter under stones in the nearby burn, but when it is very cold these will move to hibernating places we have yet to find. The small colony of toads, however, always leave the pond and spend the winter under stones or crevices nearby. The three-spined stickleback seems to vary a great deal in numbers from year to year but they grow large and the males in their breeding colours, that include a vivid red underpart and blue eyes, are spectacular. About six years ago the pond dried out completely and it took three years for the sticklebacks to recolonise the pond from the nearby burn. Palmate newts also vary in numbers whether adults or tadpoles and as regards the former they are more often than not found in the shallower, slightly warmer water. Also in the net can be found large diving beetles, water boatmen and pond snails.

Loch Maree   *15 January 1991*

My first view of the loch was from the snow-covered top of Glen Docherty and the large number of hinds near the road was a good indication that this glen is notorious for poachers of red deer. There were a few stags around, too, trying to dig down through the snow with their fore legs to get at something to graze. The huge Loch Maree was more than 4 miles (6 km) away but it still dominated the landscape and was brooded over by the snow-covered Slioch that rose above the loch to over 3000 ft (914 m). A golden eagle drifted high over the glen as I drove down to the edge of the loch, passing red deer only yards away from the road and not even bothering to look up as I went past. Most of the lochs on the way from Inverness were not only frozen but also had a layer of snow on top of the ice apart from small areas where burns entered the water. The road ran through some of the ancient remnants of Caledonian pine forest with active regeneration on the disturbed slopes of the roadside.

There was no ice or snow on Loch Maree partly because of the depth of the water and partly the 'reach' of the waves that gave almost constant motion of water. I scanned the north side of the loch with a telescope and picked out small groups of wild goats with a few of the more unusual colour form of pale brown and white. Some were feeding on gorse in open areas, others were feeding on something I could not make out along the shoreline, whilst others were in woodland no doubt browsing on young trees. In contrast, a group of six black and white goats were on a very steep slope where they are so sure-footed but likely to do damage to the vulnerable cliff ledge plants. One group of goats were sharing the grazing of a grassy slope with several red deer stags and for some reason all the animals looked up as two ravens passed over and I could only think that the birds had called, as they were just too far away for me to have heard them.

The purpose of my visit was to count the mountain hares and wild goats but as is often the case with wildlife something entirely different made the day and in this case it was the birds of prey. However by lunchtime I had no idea of what was to happen as I sat on the river bank in sunshine, although the time of year was reflected in the fact that the dipper that was singing in front of me was standing on a layer of ice that reached out in the calmer waters of the river. On a steep bank in front of me, characteristically on a south-facing slope that catches as much sun as possible, sat eight mountain hares in their white winter coats and behind me were two groups of wild goats.

I had seen the first bird of prey an hour before, circling high over a snow-capped ridge and I had to look hard to make sure it was a buzzard and not a golden eagle, as it seemed a strange place for a buzzard to be. I could only presume it was after carrion such as a red deer carcase. After a sandwich I decided to stalk the nearest mountain hare and was soon in a position when I expected it to run and I could take a photograph of the hare in motion. To say the least I was surprised when the hare simply turned and ran into a hole behind it and out of sight!

The next bird of prey was a kestrel hovering over the dark moorland and then later a sparrow-hawk that twisted through the trees in birch woodland almost like the flight of a woodcock. In contrast, I was not prepared for the next bird as it flew in front of me, and binoculars revealed a goshawk. The origin of the present population in Britain is open to debate, with some people believing that they are all from escaped falconers' birds, but to me it is irrelevant as it looked magnificent as it flew over the woodland. The last bird of prey was a male kestrel peering down from a telegraph pole where it sat looking for food below.

A telephone call told me of a wildcat that had ended up as a road casualty on the Black Isle just north of Inverness but both my informant and I were dubious about the authenticity of the dead animal. A similar call from Strathpeffer a few years ago had informed me that the farmer had shot a wildcat which had 'killed a few laying hens in a single week'. This was before the current protection under the Wildlife and Countryside Act but when I reached the farm even I was surprised to find an enormous black and white cat! The cat was sent off to an expert on wildcats and it turned out that the animal was likely to be a hybrid between a feral cat and a 'true' wildcat. This, then, is the problem as so much hybridisation has taken place in the last decade or so that the future of a pure strain of wildcat in Britain must be in doubt.

As far as the Munlochy specimen was concerned, the informant had taken the animal off the road and put it behind a tree so that it would not get flattened by more vehicles. An assignation on the Kessock Bridge eventually led me to the site of the casualty and we stood looking down at the cat which was impressively like a wildcat. The markings on the head and flanks were typical of a wildcat and the tail had the characteristic bands, a blunt tip and was about half the length of the body. Even in death it was impressive with the large yellow eyes still having that intensity of colour and the mouth was half open showing white fangs and a bright red tongue. I had forgotten how impressive were the long white whiskers. Twenty years ago, when I was warden at Inverpolly National Nature Reserve on the Ross-shire/Sutherland border, if you saw a wildcat it was likely to be just that but since then the situation has changed dramatically. A decrease in persecution and an increase in numbers and range of the wildcat are important factors, as has been the increase in afforestation that the wildcats have utilised.

On 1 April 1973 the use of the gin trap became illegal in Scotland; ironically it became illegal in England several years before. Now nearly 20 years later and against a background of poisoning, illegal snaring and trapping and egg collecting there are still gin traps in use in the Highlands. The latest incident was in mid January near Kiltarlity, a few miles west of Inverness, when a weak and exhausted pine marten was found in a gin trap. It was caught by one of its fore legs and one of the reasons for its exhaustion was that the gin trap had been insecurely fastened and, judging by the scratch marks on the trap, it had been dragged for some distance. As if indicating the pine marten's weakness it made no attempt to bite at the person who found it and released it and although obviously weak it managed to run off on release.

It is difficult to judge the feelings and principles of a person who would lay such an illegal trap which was banned because it caused so much suffering. The person would have known that not only is such a trap illegal but also that it traps indiscriminately, taking a range of mammals from fox to badger and a range of birds from buzzard to tawny owl. I made enquiries with the Chief Inspector of the SSPCA in Inverness who confirmed that this was not an isolated incident as there had been others in recent years, including three gin traps set at Loch Ness-side. The three traps had been put down to trap foxes but when a member of the public found them one contained a buzzard.

The biggest problem about the poisoning, trapping and egg collecting in the Highlands is that with vast areas containing few people the chance of seeing illegal incidents is remote. This means that the number of rare and protected species, whether mammals or birds, that we do find is just the tip of the iceberg. Who are these people who consider themselves above the law?

Weatherwise I was informed it was the best day for two months as in early March this year I stepped on to the main island of Hirta and walked up to the old village passing Soay sheep – both rams and ewes – which grazed unconcerned at my presence. I stopped to photograph one ewe that was grazing about 10 ft (3 m) off the ground on one of the larger cleitean. Soay sheep numbers on St Kilda, on the island of Hirta where they were introduced and the original island of Soay, have peaks and troughs in their populations. As forecast for this spring by people studying the sheep on Hirta the 'crash' in numbers had started, as over 30 dead sheep had already been found.

As I walked the old 'main street' of the village chattering starlings called from the walls and the occasional few notes from the St Kilda wren were as noisy as ever. Stiff-winged fulmars glided effortlessly past me and these birds that the St Kildans prized so much for their oil, feathers and meat are increasingly using the tops of walls and cleitean as breeding sites. One of the objects of my visit was to photograph some of the display panels set up by the National Trust for Scotland in one of the old houses the Trust had refurbished. Of all the exhibits the small one on the great auk was to me significant as I have always been intrigued at this long extinct species that was flightless. There was a black and white photograph of the bird – presumably a mounted specimen rather than a drawing – and underneath a model of an egg that very much resembles a larger version of a common guillemot's egg. The last great auk seen in Britain is reputed to have been taken in 1840 by the St Kildans on one of the island's great stacs – Stac an Armin – that rises abruptly from the sea in the shape of a gigantic serrated tooth. It was brought into the village by the St Kildans and later killed because it was thought to be a witch!

The loch lay silent apart from the hiss of the rain as it hit the otherwise calm surface whilst the backcloth of snow-capped hills was partly hidden by the mist that hung over the steep slopes like a shroud. There were no birds to be seen on the water or on the surrounding bleak moorland and I had turned to go when the eerie wailing of a diver made me turn back. At first I could not see the bird and then out of the mist at the far side of the loch came a black-throated diver. It had that characteristic shape of a large body with neck and head held slightly downwards. It flew round several times, calling as it went in and out of the mist, and sometimes I could not quite decide where it would appear next. At one point I thought it was going to land but it went into a tight curve, stopped wailing, and then it was gone into the mist and never re-appeared. The silence covered the scene again as if the incident had never happened.

The loch is one of the black-throated diver's breeding sites and it lays its eggs on the edge of one of the larger islands along with a small colony of common gulls. As with many other divers' nests in the Highlands, however, it suffers from fluctuating water levels, disturbance by people and predation by such things as hooded crows and foxes. Last year torrential rain wiped out eggs and chicks of all the common gulls and the black-throated divers as the main island was completely covered with a few inches of water. We can do very little with disturbance and predators but we can, ironically, do something about the elements, as in March this year an artificial, floating island was moored near the usual breeding site on the loch. These artificial islands are constructed so that they look very natural – more than one fisherman has been fooled by them – and as they float up and down with fluctuating water levels it is hoped that this particular pair of black-throated divers will be more successful in the future. The artificial islands have been a success story in recent years.

It took me a long time to realise why so many mountain hares die on Highland roads when there is prolonged snow lying on open moorland. The reason is that the hares start using the roads to move around as it is much easier to walk on the roads than it is on the heather moorland. In some areas such as the A9 south of Inverness dozens of dead hares can be seen on the higher sections of the road and over the average winter hundreds are killed by vehicles on such roads. To a lesser extent red deer will do the same and at present there is a debate on what to do about the red deer over the Drumochter Pass on the A9 about 40 miles (64 km) south of Inverness. At this time of year hundreds of red deer stags gather near this busy road and some will wander on to the roadside verges where accidents can occur.

After the last snowfall I went up into the birch wood behind the house and followed an old track probably formerly used by horse and cart. As is often the case with tracks we consider are there for our own use, wild animals had been using it to the extent that it looked more like a thoroughfare through the trees. At least two roe deer had walked the track and there were tracks of rabbits, brown hare and fox all intermingled; it was intriguing to think who was after what in the predator/prey scene. Further up in the wood I visited all the badger setts but there was no sign of overnight activity although there were two small piles of bedding waiting to go into one entrance. Badgers do not hibernate although their activities during the winter months are much reduced. I well remember last winter when tracks in our paddock indicated where a badger had sniffed around the hutch with the geese in before wandering off. That same night a fox had approached the quail shed but found no way in whilst the tracks of a single pine marten were over every hutch in the paddock.

The view from the top of Glen Docherty was spectacular, as far below to the west the shimmering Loch Maree was brooded over by the hills of Beinn Eighe and Slioch. A buzzard soaring over the nearby cliff completed the scene as I drove down the glen and then past the old Caledonian pinewood to the boat house. It had been a long time since I had been out in a boat and I had forgotten that almost child-like thrill of the smell of the engine and the lapping of the water against the prow as we headed towards our destination: Isle Maree. Unlike the other islands on the loch which are mainly covered with ancient pinewood Isle Maree is a mixture of mainly broadleaved trees. The island had been a sacred place of the Druids who are said to have introduced the oak and when St Maelrubha arrived in the seventh century he is said to have planted the holly. The larch are of more recent origin having probably colonised from the policies of the local estate; one dangerous tree that had been felled recently had growth rings indicating it was about 160 years old.

The circular dyke on the island is reputed to be the remains of a chapel and there is also an old burial ground and nearby an old decaying tree – the penny tree I had come to see. The neighbouring filled-in well was for centuries a place of pilgrimage as it cured people of mental disorders. The wishing tree demanded an offering such as a piece of clothing or a coin and so the penny tree came into being. I compared the tree with photographs I had taken ten years ago: it had not changed and as there was no room for fresh coins, they had been placed in neighbouring trees. There were also many coins lying around on the ground but they and the ones in the trees are quite safe as legend has it that death will befall anyone who takes any item from the island. I took more photographs of the penny tree to look for any changes I might have missed and then I left a coin of my own in one of the trees and made a wish.

The glen was being battered by strong winds carrying first sleet then hailstones, and the combination did little to abate my fears as I scrambled over large, wet, moss-covered boulders to reach the cave. I have always been afraid of the dark and of caves and the only reason for my visit was to see two natterers bats that were reputed to be roosting there. The entrance was narrow and I went in feet first not really knowing where my feet were going to land and then suddenly I was in the cave and its darkness. The previous month the two bats had been about 3 ft (1 m) up in a narrow slit in the rock but now there was not a single bat to be seen. They could easily have still been there as there were so many places that we could not see into despite torches but there was other equally fascinating wildlife.

Not the least of this was a single small tortoiseshell butterfly resting on the smooth surface of the large rock, whilst nearby was a herald moth which, like the butterfly, was using the cave to hibernate. Then there were the large cave spiders; I was informed later that they were *Meta menardi* which is not very common in the Highlands. The most remarkable aspect of this cave spider are the cocoons that hold the mass of pinkish eggs, small balloon-shaped structures of whitish silk suspended from the roof. We saw about a dozen of them although there could have been many more out of sight. Despite the fascination of the wildlife in the cave spiders are my third fear and the remark that some people could get into a cave but could not get out did not help allay my anxiety. It was with some relief that I jumped back into the daylight and fresh air with the fears soon forgotten as I realised how remarkable it had been despite the absence of the bats.

Before we left the glen we looked at a cat that a colleague had found as a road casualty the night before. It looked like a wildcat but it was almost certainly a hybrid as the tail was too long.

Doocotes (cotes) are found in a wide variety of places in the Highlands although they are normally associated with large houses. My latest 'find' of a cote was on an otherwide routine drive to the coast east of Inverness. The cote was a field from the road and I very nearly missed seeing it as I was negotiating a bend at the time. There was great excitement as I drove down the nearby track hoping to find someone who would give me permission to have a closer look and even take photographs. As I passed the cote I was intrigued and a little disturbed to see scaffolding round the outside and I wondered if it was facing ruin. Fortunately the gamekeeper was nearby and we had a long talk about rearing pheasants and problems with predators such as polecat ferrets, mink and pine martens. There was no problem about looking at and photographing the cote and I was more than pleased to be told that it was being dismantled and completely rebuilt.

What is fascinating about the cotes in the Highlands is that no two that I have tracked down have been the same. At Grangehall the coursing was decorated and outlined with small chips of stone piercing the mortar and known as galletting. The cote, built circa 1800, was hexagonal and at the top of each wall the pigeon entrance holes pierced half-moon-shaped stone slabs.The rat ledge – to keep rats out – was about 3 ft (1 m) down from the eaves and continuous right round the cote, and in front of the entrance holes the ledge broadened out as a landing platform for the pigeons.

In the past both adult pigeons and their young (called 'peesers' in Scotland and 'squabs' in England) would have been eaten and they could supply meat in the winter when other food was not available. The other useful by-product was the dung that was rich in potassium nitrate and which, if mixed with black earth and sulphur, produced a form of gunpowder.

A few weeks ago the local farmer told me he had seen a small brown animal dart across the road where I park the car at the side of the house. It was too big to be a weasel and too small to be a pine marten or polecat ferret so it was a mystery. When we discussed it we ruled out the obvious – a stoat – as this far north they always turn white in winter, although they always keep the black tip to the tail. Towards the end of January the mystery was solved as I was sitting at the word processor with my usual view of the bird table in the foreground and the snow-covered hills on the opposite side of the strath. The chaffinches, greenfinches and tits suddenly scattered off the bird table and as I looked out there was a stoat on the ground beneath the table; it darted up a fence post and on to the table. It was in a typical summer coat, brown above with creamy white under-parts, with the usual black tip to the tail. Tip is in fact a misnomer as about a third of the 3 in (8 cm) tail was black. Two things were intriguing: why was it in summer colours when all the other stoats I have seen in this area this winter have been white, or ermine as it is called? The second point was what it was doing on the bird table as all the birds had flown and were chattering away at their displeasure of being denied their feed. Binoculars revealed that it was feeding on soft bill food put out for blackbirds and thrushes.

Reference books revealed that normally stoats in the northern part of their range turn white but there are exceptions which can be linked with weather conditions. This has been the coldest winter with more prolonged ice and snow than we can remember for many years so why was the stoat brown? The fact that it had not turned white and that it was feeding on food on the bird table indicated it may well not have been in good condition. The situation will be watched closely as last time we had a stoat in the garden it was taking six hen's eggs a day!

The little auk was found in one of the main streets in Inverness and came to me via the environmental health department. I had forgotten just how small – one bird book likened them to the size of a starling – and dumpy these auks are and as I examined it I tried to think of what its breeding grounds were like in the high Arctic. Breeding numbers are in millions with some colonies containing over 100,000 birds – a contrast with a pavement outside a fast-food shop in the capital of the Highlands. The black and white bird looked in good health and I was tempted simply to take it to the firth from where no doubt recent blizzards had made it disorientated. But to make sure I placed it in a darkened box and went to the nearest shop for a tin of sardines and I thought it was appropriate to buy the ones in oil. My last experience of sardines was many years ago when I led Brathay expeditions to south-east Iceland and I had forgotten that characteristic and powerful smell of the small fish. The little auk went into the bath at home where it ate some of the sardines and it seemed quite happy as its tiny black webbed feet propelled it through the clear water and there was even a little wing stretching and flapping. It spent the night in the box and was fed the next morning before I set off for the firth near Inverness.

This small incident pales before the recent mortality of sea birds along the east coast of Britain with thousands being found round the coasts of the Highlands alone. There are many theories for the masses of birds found dead but overfishing by ourselves seems to be the likeliest reason. But there were plenty of fish in the Beauly Firth and quite unprecedented numbers of sea birds were feeding on them. I gently placed the little auk into the water and it swam out from the shoreline and sat for a moment looking at me. Then it dived and emerged a few feet further out and as I watched it swim away there were tears in my eyes.

The route to this east-coast lighthouse took me through attractively named villages such as Arabella, Hill of Fearn and Portmahomack, the latter still having a disused ice house in the middle of the village. Fields around these villages attract large wintering flocks of greylag geese and whooper swans and I was not disappointed. One field held 71 whooper swans, most of them asleep, but of the herd only six were juveniles so the breeding success in Iceland last year had been low. Only two fields further on there were around 30 greylag geese but I could not stop to count accurately as there was a bad bend in the road. When I first came along this road 15 years ago there seemed to be corn buntings in every suitable field with their call notes, which resemble jangling keys, carrying some distance. Sadly these dumpy-looking birds have not been in the area for some years and this has been a similar story elsewhere in the Highlands. Just before Tarbatness there were two more interesting birds: a covey of five grey partridges in the corner of a field and then near the sea 41 rock doves and, as usual, although the majority were pure-looking there was one very dark bird and another that was almost white.

Lunch was taken at the end of the peninsula whilst watching male and female eider ducks bobbing around on the waves with herring gulls nearby waiting for scraps as the ducks started to feed under water. The drake eiders were in their fine breeding plumage and the apple-green coloured feathers on their heads were conspicuous in the weak sunshine. I fully expected to hear their attractive cooing call notes but they did not oblige. On the shoreline I picked up five small stones from the beach and played the game 'five stones' which I have not done or seen done for more years than I care to remember. Then the excitement of the day in the form of a single cowrie shell with the three pale brown spots indicating it was the European cowrie – *Trivia monacha*.

I have looked for cowries in various parts of the Highlands and found some of the best places have been at John o'Groats up on the north coast of Caithness and a very small beach on the Ardnamurchan peninsula west of Fort William. In contrast small rock pools on the South Side Nature Trail on the Isle of Rum had so few cowries that it sometimes took me a very long time to find even one specimen. There is also a tiny area in which to find cowries at Balnakeil Bay in north-west Sutherland, although that splendid area has now been spoilt by a golf course on the machair that has interesting swarms of orchids and the exquisite Scottish primrose.

What was interesting about the Balnakeil site was that you could only look for the cowries at low water so it was always a case of checking tide tables before we set out. Unfortunately the drive north up the western parts of Sutherland means that you pass through very large areas that have been overgrazed by sheep and deer as well as overburnt for a very long time. The degradation caused is almost awesome.

Cowrie Shells

There may not be any true wilderness left in the Highlands but I saw plenty of wildness towards the end of February on the coastline of Wester Ross. The purpose of my visit was to photograph the old ice house at Badentarbat and the small lochan from where they gathered the ice. But typical of the Highlands, especially at this time of year, I had to wait for the weather for just under half an hour. Rain, sleet and snow fell during that period and I almost gave up but then there was a five-minute sunny break and the black and white photographs were quickly taken. Behind me to the north-east lay the snow-capped peaks of that dramatic range of hills such as Coigach, Stac Polly, Cul Mor and Cul Beag and then to the north of these massifs my favourite hill – Suilven – looking as dramatic as ever as if guarding all the other hills by its sheer size. In the other direction lay the marine island of Tanera Mor and I thought of one of my mentor's days there – the late Sir Frank Fraser Darling. Then, years ago, my own few visits when I would purchase stamps to send the mail off the island with some very attractive natural history designs that I do not think have been matched by the General Post Office, but perhaps I am biased.

The ice house at Badentarbat had catered for the salmon of the netting station nearby and there was even a shed in which to hang the nets. The netsman's house looked occupied but the netting station had gone and all that was left apart from the buildings were remains of the old winches and the dilapidated wooden pier. Later in the year the lochan used for gathering ice would echo to the guttural calls of a breeding colony of toads, but for now the scene was stolen by three ringed plovers on the short-cropped turf just away from the splash zone of the sea. It looked as if two males were trying to attract the attention of a single female so I left them to it and motored down to nearby Achnahaird Bay to look for great northern divers.

Most of my mistakes in wildlife terms are from wrong identification or wrongly assuming things; this often happens simply because my full-time job is as a wildlife conservationist and it is also my hobby. Whatever the reason for my mistake earlier this month I was really annoyed with myself. The visit to the strath had started well with seeing a golden eagle high over the River Findhorn and a raven flying off a cliff face and trying to make up its mind whether the eagle was worth mobbing. A huge billy goat was under the birch trees and for some reason it looked really aggressive although I could see no other goats nearby. Its long black horns rose almost parallel as opposed to the outward-curved horns characteristic of most of the tribe of goats living in this strath. These sightings were made that much more memorable because of the backcloth of the snow-covered hills.

The regrettable incident happened when I was halfway back down the strath driving along the very narrow road. I was driving very slowly when I realised that there was a blackish nanny grazing just above the road. She was facing me and as I glanced towards her I suddenly realised that 3 ft (1 m) away from her was a mountain hare; I could just see the white fur of its back. I knew from my own experience that these two mammals readily accept each other's presence so I parked the vehicle further on and walked slowly back with camera at the ready. When I was several yards away the nanny suddenly looked up and snorted at me and backed off a few yards and then I realised my mistake. The so-called mountain hare was a white kid that had just been born and the afterbirth was still hanging out of the nanny. All thoughts of a photograph went as I retreated rapidly, calling myself some names at disturbing the nanny at such a critical time. Fortunately I had only gone a few yards before the nanny was back at the kid and carrying on as if nothing had happened.

A telephone caller queried why animals had spent the night in a hut circle just north of Inverness where tracks in the snow indicated that a large number of animals had been involved. The caller thought they might be deer and when I walked the fields later that day I found many tracks converging on the stones but I was not prepared for what I found. There were many tracks within the circle of stones but then immediately next to a huge stone several feet high and across and about 6 in (15 cm) thick was an amazing sight. For about three-quarters of an acre there were so many tracks that I could not find a 6 in (15 cm) square devoid of tracks or droppings. All the tracks were made by brown hares – the altitude is too low for mountain hares – and it was obvious that a large number of hares had been involved.

Reference books mention that elsewhere gatherings of brown hares have been seen in the past with up to 40 animals involved. The mystery is why such gatherings take place, although one suggestion is that it gives the males the chance to show off to the females. But this gathering took place with 8 in (20 cm) of snow on the ground and it was obvious that the hares had travelled some distance for whatever ceremony was involved. Brown hares are so mysterious that I would not be surprised if the location had something to do with the ancient hut circle but there may be a simpler explanation. If you took away local conifer plantations then from the raised mound on which the hut circle stood there would be commanding views of the strath. This would enable hares to see each other moving towards the site and once they were there any predators such as foxes could be seen from a long way off. In such deep snow hare tracks are one of the few that can be recognised; badgers are another as their short legs mean that their chests form a broad furrow between their footprints.

Keeping poultry these days can be difficult with the apparent increase in numbers and distribution of predators. In the last week someone further up the strath had lost four geese and he called in to see me and ask advice. He was convinced it was a pine marten and this was based on the fact that he had seen one and in any case pieces of the dead birds had been taken up into trees. I often get such queries and the very first thing I ask is whether the poultry are put into strong hutches every night. In this case the dozen geese had simply been left to spend the night on a nearby loch only yards away from the house. Every other morning a dead and partly eaten goose would be found in the shallows although there were no signs left by the predator.

The problem with this type of incident is that the original predator may not be the only one. I remember investigating a case on an estate near Inverness when an estimated 80 pheasant poults had been killed over three nights, almost certainly by pine martens. When I examined the carcases at the site a hooded crow and carrion crow were feeding on carcases, a buzzard nearby had obviously gorged itself and there were fresh fox spraints. As regards the geese I could only suggest a fox may have been the initial culprit with other mammals or birds taking pieces up into the trees. My recommendation was to build some sound hutches to keep the birds in overnight. Some people I know have also been 'raided' by mink and there are now several places in the Highlands where people have simply stopped keeping poultry as they have lost so many birds, with mink increasingly to blame. Stout hutches, however, are not the complete answer as in the last few years there have been increasing reports of pine martens taking poultry in daylight and they have actually been seen doing so in a number of places throughout the Highlands.

This summer will see me compiling an inventory of ice houses in the Highlands for the Archaeological Department of the Highland Regional Council. This has come about not only because of my long interest in these fascinating structures but also because one was demolished without the department's knowledge. I mentioned the demise of one of the two ice houses in Portmahomack in a previous Country Diary and I gave some old photographs of the ice house to the department as they had none and the question of an inventory arose. Sources of information on ice houses in the area are scattered, although the listed ice houses are known by various local departments. The major book on ice houses is a massive gazetteer published in 1990 but although I consulted this in the Inverness reference library it only lists 23 for the Highlands. In fact it appears that most harbours and ports have them including all round the Caithness and Sutherland coasts, let alone others closer to home. Some of the ice houses are huge structures such as the one on the Black Isle near Inverness that has two compartments, each large enough to take a small lorry. In contrast the two small ones side by side on a rock face by Beauly may be unique in their size.

The use of ice-making machines put ice houses under threat and a slight rise in temperature in Britain after 1840 meant natural ice was not readily available and had to be imported from Norway and America. With the coming of refrigerators the end of the ice houses was in sight, although it was a long time coming as ice was still being imported into Britain in the 1930s and in some remote country estates they were still in use after the Second World War. If any reader knows of any existing or demolished ice houses in the Highlands perhaps they could let me know so that the future of these structures is assured and brought to the attention of the local authorities.

Cuckoo

Spring

With the sun low over the sea the distant panorama to the west included outlines of the islands of Eigg, Rum and Skye. The only difference in lighting was on Rum as the hills that rise to over 2500 ft (762 m) were laden with snow – unusual even for this island. Some of these hills such as Hallival, Barkeval and Askival were named by the Norsemen – important landmarks for exploring and plundering this jagged west coast of Scotland. The sea was flat calm so it was easy to see the birds and seals as I waited to pick someone up off the Small Isles ferry.

Most of the activity on the sea was centred on the half-dozen grey seals that were fishing just outside the harbour wall. One cow seemed to be having difficulty with a fish that looked just under 2 ft (0.6 m) long and judging by its dark colouring could well have been a pollack. Several times the seal shook the fish violently and small pieces of fish would drop into the water only to be snapped up by the ever-present herring gulls. In the end the seal threw the remains of the fish a few inches into the air and then dived with its prey without coming back up as far as I could see. There was a lot of diving and surfacing from the other seals but they seemed to have no luck with their fishing.

Shags were also fishing but before diving they were moving across the water with heads under the surface looking for prey and then came the characteristic dive. They seemed to have mixed fortunes as from the eight birds I could see only four caught fish in the half-hour I was watching. These were small fish that I could not identify but on one occasion the nearest shag brought up a fish that looked very much like a gurnet about 5 in (13 cm) long. Herring gulls were everywhere, with many dark brown-barred immature birds which called repeatedly as if in frustration at the grey and white adults that in the main were just loafing about in pairs. These were on rocks, the pier, trawler rigging, houses and even on top of the huge ice plant. In contrast the female eider sat on the water just outside the harbour – no sign of a male – and she sat motionless until a huge bull seal surfaced a yard away and she was quickly off, only to settle on some nearby rocks amidst yet more gulls. By then the sun had gone down leaving the islands in a pale blue light, the sea mirroring everything until the ferry broke the calmness of the water.

I thought of my own trips to these islands at various times of the year, and some of the frustrating times trying to get to Rum only to have the ferry turn back because of the weather. On evenings at the right time of the year, the ferry would run through large flocks of Manx shearwaters getting ready to fly under the cover of darkness to their usual breeding sites on top of the hills. Dolphins would sometimes follow the boat for long distances, and in the summer seabirds such as gannets, puffins and the fulmars – the latter there all year round – were impressive. Although Rum has always fascinated me, the other islands have a charm of their own. I never did land on Eigg or Muck but perhaps some islands should be like that – a little mysterious, as although you went past them often enough you never did find out any of the secrets.

It was always a thrill to enter Loch Scresort on Rum and be picked up by the small ferry called the *Rhouma*. The great Kinloch Castle sat as if brooding over the sea loch, and sometimes Highland ponies would be grazing in front of the castle. To land on Rum was like entering another world and it always seemed to welcome you – apart from when the midges were out in force. At the end of the stay there was regret and sadness at having to leave, despite leaving there dozens and dozens of times. Rum has so much to offer: the Highland cattle, the famous pony stud and the red deer. There were also the quiet parts of the island where you would never meet anybody.

I passed the 'Rock Patrol' just after first light on the road running along the western shore of the loch. Each morning the driver of this car covers the road from Inverness to Fort William looking for landslides or large stones that can damage vehicles or cause accidents. It typifies the difficulties in constructing this main road along steep hillsides with any vehicle dwarfed by the steep-sided banks topped with trees. Further on I came across a more natural hazard as I had to brake hard to avoid a roe deer. The buck ran out of cover just a few yards in front of my car and then in a single bound leapt over a stone wall into more woodland. If it had been at night the near accident would probably not have happened as the enlightened estate has put reflectors on short posts on both sides of the road.

Loch Ness that morning was the calmest I can ever remember seeing and for a change it was easy to see the few birds that occur on this huge expanse of water. A group of tufted duck near the water's edge, several separate pairs of mallard no doubt with thoughts of nesting in mind, two pairs of displaying red-breasted mergansers and two pairs of Slavonian grebes. The latter were probably waiting for slightly warmer weather so that they could fly up to the hill lochs where the small Scottish population – about 70 pairs – breeds. Despite the cold there was at least some colour along the roadside and I was particularly pleased to see the first primroses in flower. Coltsfoot was well out and both birch and alder catkins brightened the scene, but all paled in contrast to the yellow pollen masses of the sallows. Circling the large alderwood at Drumnadrochit I was surprised to see no fewer than 11 roe deer in one field and nine in another – certainly the largest number of roe I have seen close together. Urquhart Castle was splendid in the morning light but despite stopping the car to scan the water as always, I could see absolutely no sign of the Loch Ness monster!

It is difficut to say which of the islands of Boreray, Stac Lee and Stac an Armin is the most impressive. They each have a character of their own and each a feature that can identify them. Stac Lee is simply a huge rock rising sheer on all sides from the sea – broader on one side than the other – whilst Stac an Armin is a jagged triangle. In contrast Boreray is much larger than either of the Stacs and has fertile-looking green areas. What they have in common are gannets that line ledges, mass in great breeding areas or utilise what flat areas there are on the tops. The three areas support around 50,000 pairs of gannets, the largest gannetry in the world, and is a spectacular wildlife scene as the birds are constantly leaving for and arriving from their feeding grounds.

One aspect that impressed me on my last visit in early June was the large number of non-breeding gannets. These were mainly adults and four-year-old birds – the latter having dark feathers on parts of their wings – with a few younger birds. The largest non-breeding groups were sitting around on the grassy slopes of Boreray and in one such group I estimated there were over 800 individuals. Many adults were returning to the colony carrying nesting material, although with eggs already in existing nests the material – sometimes coloured fish netting – could well have been a greeting display for the bird incubating the eggs. Thousands of gannets were in the air at any one time, whether diving, circling or flying purposefully out or in and the noise was incredible.

How interesting therefore, that despite the noise of all the sea birds and the waves crashing on the jagged coastline it was still easy to hear the song of the famous St Kilda wren. Perhaps part of the selection to evolve this island race was that the song had to be louder than that of mainland wrens so that it could be heard above a million sea birds.

The reason for our visit to this sessile oakwood west of Fort William was to assess various tasks carried out by volunteers from the Scottish Conservation Projects Trust. Their main task this year was to clear more trees and shrubs – mainly birch – to open up rides and glades for butterflies and other insects. Originally the aims and objects within the management plan of this National Nature Reserve were to allow the whole area to revert to high forest and areas were fenced off to exclude stock, roe deer and red deer. Then surveys showed that it was a very important area for butterflies and as these need sheltered sunspots a whole new system of rides and glades was created. Another task for the volunteers was to clear 11 small areas of bog myrtle and the thick grass litter; all these areas stood out as they were covered with the fresh green leaves of purple moor grass. But despite this the idea was working, as already the leaves of flowering plants such as bugle and heath-spotted orchids were showing. The third task was to dig two ponds for amphibians and dragonflies and there had already been signs of their success, as within a few hours of digging one of the ponds two female frogs had laid two clumps of spawn. Unfortunately most of the eggs had been killed off by subsequent frosts but it is a good sign for the future.

The wood must have one of the greatest concentrations of pine martens in the area as there were droppings everywhere, whilst beside the main burn through the wood spraints of otter could be seen. During the whole of our time in the wood there was birdsong all around including migrants such as redstarts, wood warblers, willow warblers and chiffchaffs and more resident birds such as siskins, mistle thrushes, goldcrests and chaffinches. But for me the day will be remembered for the smell of bog myrtle as time after time I crushed the tips of the twigs between my fingers and smelt that fragrance that gives it its other name of sweet gale.

After studying the chequered skipper butterfly for around 27 years it is stimulating suddenly to find considerable interest in a species that became extinct in England during the early 1970s but still occurs at about 40 sites around Fort William. On 1 June my first call was a superb oakwood several miles north of the town and there I met the Wildlife Adviser for the Economic Forestry Group. How encouraging to be able to advise on the future management of the wood with chequered skippers and butterflies in mind. Despite the need to allow regeneration and some planting, sufficient glades and rides would be maintained to allow suntraps for butterflies. We then went on to plan for a series of nestboxes with pied flycatchers in mind, a series of bat boxes and even a pond for dragonflies and amphibians.

Chequered Skipper Butterfly

To everyone's delight the sun came out just before we left and I managed to find an adult chequered skipper.

Then it was on to another sessile oakwood and here I joined a small group of entomologists who were discussing a three-year study of the chequered skipper that has just started with a grant from the Nature Conservancy Council. It was by then raining hard but the research student had previously located one of the butterflies and we saw it sitting on a leaf of purple moor grass, which is one of the food plants for its caterpillars. We walked and talked in the rain with the background music of birdsong. We discussed glades and rides again and how harmless marking of individual butterflies was helping to form a picture of the butterfly movements.

I then left the group to meet up with a young lady from BBC Radio 4 who had driven up from Edinburgh to interview me about – yes – the chequered skipper! The interview was disrupted by the midges that came out in force as the rain ceased its downpour but, as is often the case, the lack of sunshine kept the butterflies out of sight and we never did see one. I went home a much happier man but the day was marred by the observations of a lady at the first wood of the day as she told us that the week before there had been five groups of people in the wood collecting butterflies. I wonder why.

Sleep, the night before a trip to this archipelago which lies 50 miles (80 km) west of the Western Isles, is impossible as there is too much excitement in my mind. This time it was a large Super Puma helicopter that took 25 minutes to take us from Benbecula to St Kilda and there once again I was walking up that famous main street on Hirta where most of the St Kildans once lived.

The Soay sheep looked ragged with much of their wool being shed but I just had to photograph, yet again, more of the heads of the rams that are so impressive at close quarters. The spread of the fulmar into the village that I noted in this Country Diary on 20 August 1987 has continued to the upper part of the village and the first occupied nest on the floor of an open-topped cleit was found this year.

Great skuas have also spread from the first breeding record on Hirta in 1956 to 25 pairs in 1978 and this year 45 pairs. There have also been smaller numbers on the nearby island of Soay. I well remember a few years ago my biggest thrill on Hirta, which came from an incident with a pair of great skuas. I had strayed into their territory and I was being dive-bombed in the usual way. When one of the birds went close by I saw some colour on one leg. Moving to the edge of their territory, and peace and quiet, I watched the two birds land on a knoll and spied them through binoculars. One of the birds had two plastic rings on its legs, a red one and a brown one and this combination proved that I had ringed it in south-east Iceland five years before. This was the first time one of the young Icelandic birds had ever been found breeding in another colony. My visit to Hirta this time was short-lived as most of the time was spent on discussions with the summer warden, but as the helicopter once again soared up over Village Bay I could look across to Boreray, Stac Lee and Stac an Armin, white with gannets and fulmars.

It is difficult to imagine our anticipation at seeing the house martins round the house again but as May began there was that frequent listening for the characteristic twittering notes and even more frequent glances into the sky as I fed the poultry, ducks and geese of an evening. The martins are generally in the area for two to three weeks before coming to the house and they spend their time accompanying the swallows and sand martins over rivers and lochs looking for scarce insect food. Last year on the evening of 2 May amidst rain and very overcast weather they had turned up, so coming back from the office this year on the same date one can imagine our thoughts. I had just started sorting the day's eggs when the notes from the nest over the kitchen window gave them away and on going outside there were two pairs of house martins with white rumps clearly showing as they flitted from the eaves. Now there are eight or nine pairs busy rebuilding last year's nests and taking full advantage of the new, large pond that has so much mud on the margins it must be a paradise for the birds.

But they are not the only attraction in the garden as a pair of redstarts investigated the nestbox nearest to the house and then decided to use a box on a large beech tree further down the garden. Early in the morning a cock pheasant struts around the bottom of the bird table under our bedroom window as if clamouring for food to be taken down to the poultry runs. He seems to spend most of his time with the hens and ducks at the food bowls and is reluctant to leave until he has had his fill. We have not seen a hen bird but she could well be sitting on eggs in the paddock as they can be very secretive. Once again we have decided to keep the food going on the bird table throughout the summer and on 12 May with cold rain bringing a covering of snow to the tops the birds were glad of the peanuts, with about 30 greenfinches and 20 chaffinches present.

Drummossie Moor

My copy of the first edition of the Ordnance Survey map – revised to 1896 – shows an area called Drummossie Moor flanking the southern edge of Inverness and stretching for miles to the east and west. Since then the tract of moorland has slowly been fragmented although there are still large areas of very wet moorland that have survived. The broad sweep of the A9 slices through the eastern half and in parts conifers were planted, some on the drier ground but others on drained wet ground. Overgrazing and overburning have taken their toll except again for the really wet areas, although a few scattered remnants of Scots pine hang on. The moorland is so close to Inverness that within ten minutes of the centre of town you can drive over the moorland at heights up to over 800 ft (244 m). Here you can pass through a mosaic of habitats such as bog pools, lochans, wet moorland, dry grassy knolls and gorse patches and this means there is a comparative variety of birds to see. The gorse patches have resident stonechats which normally stay there all the year round and at this time of the year the adult males are resplendent in their fine breeding plumage. Drake mallard are hanging around the lochans where no doubt the females are on eggs and they are probably not far from hatching. Above them the aerial displays of lapwings have a fluttering flight which reminds me why as a lad I coined the name of 'flappers' for them.

This is the route to the office each weekday and there always seems to be something to see such as curlews planing down in their courtship flight and at dusk at the right time of year short-eared owls hunting for voles. The area is shot over by walking up red grouse whilst on the wooded southern edge pheasants are shot. We regularly see both species and it is only the presence of roadside gorse bushes that make the red grouse fly just that little bit higher so that they actually avoid the car. In the last three years we have seen

most of the birds of prey of the Highlands whilst driving this journey including peregrine, merlin – it was chasing meadow pipits –
buzzard, kestrel and osprey. The old pines are reputed to support
crested tits and capercaillie but our only venture off the road in
search of these birds nearly ended in disaster as we kept sinking into
the bog pools. Long may it remain so to stop further exploitation.

Merlin

Gorse bushes covered with bright yellow flowers flanked the edge of the loch and dominated the one island from where a willow warbler was singing. There was so much bird activity on and around the loch that it was difficult to concentrate on one aspect but I suppose the Slavonian grebes were the main attraction. T.A. Coward's three volumes so admirably edited into one volume by J.A.G. Barnes in 1969 has a wonderful description of them as having:

> erectile horns that are tufts of chestnut feathers, extending from the eye and projecting above the nape: some of these are long and silky in texture and look golden or straw-yellow in sunlight. The neck and back in summer are deep chestnut, coppery in strong light, the cheeks and chin are velvet black and there is a full tippet, shorter than that of a great crested grebe and frequently expanded. When swimming away from the observer, glancing over its shoulder, the bird shows a yellow nape divided by a dark line.

I cannot think of a better description but we saw all these features and more with the telescope. There were five, possibly six pairs of these grebes and there were at least two pairs of little grebes and at one stage in one field of view I could see a Slavonian grebe and little grebe each struggling with a small trout within 3 ft (1 m) of each other.

On a more sombre note there was a family party of greylag geese with two birds with trailing wings from hitting overhead cables whilst a solitary whooper swan, feeding at the water's edge, had a similar wing injury. Fights were breaking out between coot and moorhens and coot and mallard, in both cases the coot easily came out on top, perhaps because the other birds had strayed too close to its nest. Two female mallard had broods of two and three ducklings still very small and I wondered what predator had so quickly reduced their ranks. Meanwhile sand martins swept low over the water, black-headed gulls made short dives into the water more like terns and were coming up with something about an inch long. A lapwing, sitting tight on its nest near the water's edge, and oystercatcher, coot and mallard were feeding within yards whilst a male and female goosander swam past – line astern.

This is one of the better lochs for birds near Inverness and fortunately, with the road running along the edge of two sides, a car can conveniently be used as a hide. The end result is a closer view of the birds without disturbing them. The loch holds brown trout and it is fished every summer by anglers who at certain times of the year are in competition with visiting ospreys and resident herons. Just occasionally cormorants turn up, and I am always surprised there are not more as the loch is fairly close to the sea. A few of one of my favourite ducks turns up at this time of year, namely the gadwall, with the female looking a little like a female mallard. The male has grey flanks and a black stern, but these features are not conspicuous and you often have to look twice at these birds. A few gadwell nest in the Highlands but the main cluster is in the flow country of Caithness.

My favourite duck of this loch, however is undoubtedly the wigeon, hundreds of which overwinter there, only leaving the loch when it is iced over and then they go into the nearby firths. Wigeon always seem to be talking to each other as there is a constant calling from the water and the air as small flocks wheel over the water and then suddenly descend. The males have a conspicuous white bar on their wings when in flight. I always hope that some of these birds will stay and breed in the Highlands but I should imagine that most of them return to Scandinavia to nest.

The River Findhorn lay below me with a scattering of wild goats lying down along its bank – nannies, billies and this year's kids together – set against a background of oystercatchers piping away whilst their partners sat on eggs in the grassy fields. The red deer stags were in velvet and two of the larger specimens were up on their hind legs boxing like brown hares. Any fighting that could damage the velvet covered antlers was unwise as it could be long-lasting damage so they resort to boxing. The hinds were on the higher ground the other side of the strath and I scanned the hillside with the telescope hoping to see a newborn calf but it was not to be – just the hinds in loose small groups as if wanting the calving to be over for another summer. A dipper called from the fast-flowing river

Lesser Celandine

as if annoyed at the angler who walked up the far bank, whilst a red-breasted merganser was disturbed – its white wing patches flashed in the sun as it flew below me.

There seemed to be so much to see from the car that I had to force myself out and up the small burn; over to the right a large white billy with well-curved horns refused to be moved and as I went downwind of him that typical goat smell was very strong indeed. The burn water was as clear as crystal and a joy to drink as pearl-bordered fritillaries fluttered past and a ring ouzel called from a small cliff where no doubt it was nesting. A few yards further on I watched one of the fritillaries that must have just emerged as the wings were perfect and rich brown, with the insect lethargic even in the strong sunshine.

Then I was away from the bubbling of the river far below me as I walked into a tiny corrie where even the burn made no noise. The magical silence of the Highlands overtook me and I sat on a large stone next to the water's edge where the first starry saxifrages were in flower with their white petals touched with a yellow spot. For several minutes there was complete silence and then it was broken by a meadow pipit's call as if in response to the male cuckoo calling from the woodland below. I went reluctantly back to the car, being scolded by the ring ouzel on the way and I felt as if I had invaded a small private world of wildlife – a thought that often comes to me when I experience that silence of the Highlands that can be comforting, magical and sometimes disturbing.

At the beginning of June this year more rain fell in two days than in the whole of May and it proved disastrous for the nesting black-throated divers. The rapid rise in water levels simply washed away eggs from many nests as these are located close to the water's edge so that the sitting diver can shuffle into the water. Legs of divers are set so far back on their body that whilst they are a very useful and powerful means of swimming the bird has great difficulty walking upright. The loss of eggs is in itself significant but as important was the late date of the downpour as it means that few divers, if any, will have time to lay a second clutch this year. One or two chicks had fortunately already hatched and may have survived but the main hope for the year lies in the fate of those divers that nested on artificial floating islands. These moored islands rise and fall as the water levels fluctuate, but up until this year such islands had not been very successful and the very few divers using them had almost led to the scheme being abandoned. Fortunately this year the scheme has been far more successful, as out of 23 artificial islands no fewer that eight are being used by black-throated divers and one by a red-throated diver.

However apart from the fluctuating water levels these rare birds – there are fewer than 100 breeding pairs in Britain – have other problems. Predators, for example, include not only hooded crows but also otters, although the extent of such predation is not known. A photographer in a hide saw a black-throated diver disturbed by an otter that promptly ate the two eggs in the nest scrape. In another case on open water an otter rose underneath an adult diver and tried to take the bird but was disturbed, although the diver was later found dead on the shoreline. Perhaps the most unusual record, however, came earlier this year when evidence pointed to the fact that red deer had trampled on the two eggs in a nest.

Sutherland is unusual in that the low east coast is bounded by the North Sea whilst its west and north coasts are high and irregular and form the great Atlantic seaboard. Recently I was standing under a cliff a few miles inland from the east coast where ramsons were in flower and a pearl-bordered fritillary fluttered in the small sunlit glade amidst the dense shade of the birch trees. A buzzard mewed overhead as it passed down the strath no doubt looking for rabbits, whilst on the cliff in front of me were the bright white flowers of starry saxifrage. Nearby an eggshell had given away a teal's nest, as there in the clumps of feathers were the remains of about ten eggs from a successful hatching. The site was a good 50 yds (46 m) from water and near the base of the cliff and the shallow, feather lined cup was under a heather clump. Strath Fleet is one of the softer and greener straths with even the cliffs not looking cold and stark, although the general feeling came more from the small fields through which the river flowed.

What made the scene, however, were dozens of fulmars dotted over the cliff on their breeding ledges and so far from the sea. I have seen fulmars far inland in Iceland where their colony was several miles over a glacier with the ice front itself also several miles from the sea. The adults, and later the young, had an added problem in getting to the sea as they had to run the gauntlet of a few hundred pairs of great skuas. In the strath the unusual habit – for Britain – of nesting well inland started in the early 1950s probably because, with the gradual spread of the fulmar and the fact that there are few ideal sea cliffs along this low coastline, they had no alternative but to go inland. Interestingly, fulmars have been increasingly found in the prey items at a golden eagle eyrie well inland in Sutherland and the adult eagles could only have obtained them by flying through other eagle territories to the sea or an even longer journey to Strath Fleet.

The fishing boats in their bright colours of blue, green, brown and grey lay partly on their sides as they had been dragged up the narrow strip of yellow sand at the end of the loch. We walked along the path under the birch trees which were showing spring green leaves and at least two willow warblers were singing. With such a strong wind it felt much better as we went quietly into the hide and there was some satisfaction as we found we had the place to ourselves. A quick glance through binoculars revealed a single drake mallard upending in a gap in the sedge bed and I was about to comment on the lack of birds when as if by a signal round a corner swam a pair of Slavonian grebes. Within ten minutes they were feeding directly in front of the hide and we could see every detail of their attractive plumage – even the red eyes. Another pair appeared from the same direction as the first and then the telescope picked up another pair on the far bank and yet another pair to our right. There was virtually no display from any of the pairs and this may well have been because of the conditions as the wind seemed to swirl in every direction over the loch and the long golden 'horn' feathers were being flapped around.

Other birds included a male reed bunting that was feeding in the sedge bed; a single grey wagtail flew past and there were chaffinches everywhere in the birch trees. We were intrigued at the open-fronted nestbox near the hide as it had a very narrow slit as an entrance; further off we could see a nest box designed for goldeneye ducks. In this particular area these boxes are often colonised by tawny owls, which reminded me that I was sent an interesting record last week of such a box near Fort William that has been taken over by a barn owl which is a rare species in the Highlands. The highlight of our visit was meeting the RSPB summer warden who was very helpful and informative and we wished her luck.

There is something wrong with the black-headed gull colonies in parts of the Highlands and nobody is quite sure of the reasons. It came to a head last year when several well-known and relatively old colonies were simply deserted and as far as we know the birds just inspected the sites and left without even attempting to nest. I looked at a small number of breeding colonies of these attractive gulls and found what I believed to be the reason at the time: the water levels at the sites were so low that any predators such as a fox could simply have walked out to the nests and helped themselves to eggs or chicks. As if proving this theory the one colony where the birds appeared to be in their usual numbers was on a lochan where the nests were in such a situation amongst reeds that any fluctuation in water levels would have made no difference.

This spring the rainfall has been 'normal' with water levels well up and so it was with some anticipation that we visited the gull colonies. The two colonies not far from home that had been completely deserted last year were particularly interesting as at one site the birds were late attempting to settle in and by the end of the first week in May there were only 15 pairs – less than half the usual number.

At the other colony in Strathdearn there were no birds on the actual breeding site but there were a few birds flying up the strath as if uncertain what to do although to my, no doubt untrained, eye the water levels looked similar to what they had been in previous years. About ten years ago there was a view that black-headed gulls were decreasing in numbers but there seemed to be no total desertion of colonies. What slim evidence there is suggests that food may be the problem and yet it is difficult to see just what changes in land use have taken place to lower the food resources for such gulls. A mystery indeed.

It rained all day as we drove up the east coast north of Inverness, but the Highlands scenery was still impressive as the mist and rain swirled round the hills and the lochs were so dark that they seemed to brood over the moorland. Fulmars were on their inland cliffs at the Mound near Golspie and all along the coast the female eiders had broods of ducklings. Our destination was Berriedale and we wrongly thought that the new Dornoch Bridge was open which is why we ended up in the village of Edderton where in the small shop we found to our surprise and pleasure corn dollies on sale. Unlike further south the use and tradition of corn dollies do not seem to have been so widespread in the Highlands.

Further north at Berriedale we were meeting up with the factor of the Welbeck Estate who had promised to show us some mounted specimens of the black form of the mountain hares in Langwell House.The melanistic form is very rare in Britain but at the beginning of this century no fewer than 15 had been shot in this south-east corner of Caithness. Having read so much about these hares and having waited so long to see one it was with great anticipation that we opened the door of the room. There were five of the black hares in glass cases, including one case with a hare in typical white winter coat in contrast to the black hare next to it. One of the specimens had been deliberately shot in February to see whether this black form changed into the white winter coat; it was still black. Other mounted specimens in this 'Victorian Room' included wildcats, pine martens and badger.

If this was not enough we then looked at the herd of white fallow deer that had been originally introduced into the small deer park in about 1900. These fallow deer are not as hardy as the native roe and red deer despite the series of mild winters that have been the reason for both the native species expanding their range and numbers.

The first fishing foray after brown trout is always filled with excitement and anticipation and ours came early in April. It was our first time on this particular loch despite the fact that it is only a few minutes away on the other side of the village of the same name. In one part of the boathouse there were the remains of a swallows' nest from last year whilst in the cladding on the face outside was – neatly tucked away in a crevice – the old nest of a tree creeper. After finding the right oars and tying on the rollocks – I have known them to fall out at the most inconvenient moments – we slid the boat into the water and as it surged against the ripple of the water I thought of *The Wind in the Willows*. We decided to go against the breeze right up to the other end of the loch and I was pleased at not feeling the strain, for the traditional clinker boat was heavy and the distance half a mile which I rowed without stopping.

Halfway up the loch we heard the first faint croaking and then in the far end we actually saw them: the first was a bundle of male toads fighting to clasp on to a single female. Then there were single males everywhere we looked, obviously just swimming around looking for females. We were to find them or hear them almost everywhere we looked, although they were mainly on the margins where the submerged vegetation grew. In the Highlands we tend just to accept frogs and toads, especially the former as they are so widespread, and it is sad to hear how the numbers have been so reduced further south. But this breeding colony of toads in Loch Farr was exciting by any standards because of its sheer size. As we left – needless to say fishless – we stopped to move two live toads off the road at the east end of the loch and we noted two flattened ones. Fortunately, despite the number of toads at this colony there is little likelihood of large numbers of road casualties as the very narrow road is seldom used by traffic.

Several years ago I visited a series of pools near Inverness that held a strong population of great crested newts and my presumption at the time was that these newts had been introduced either accidentally or deliberately. The reason for this theory was that after the Second World War pet shops throughout Scotland sold all three species of newts – the other two being palmate and smooth – and many escaped or the owners became tired of them and let them loose. The pools in question are beside a large school and schools often used to keep animals such as newts for biology lessons. Since my visits to these pools, however, other records have come in to me such as a curling pond to the east of Inverness and a large loch in the same direction and another curling pond to the west. Then earlier this month I gave a talk on mountain hares and brown hares to an

Pygmy Shrew

audience in the Inverness Museum and afterwards a lady came up to me and asked if I was interested in the fact that she had great crested newts in her garden, adjacent to a large loch to the west of Inverness. I took down the details and then did a literature search for more records.

The distribution atlas shows a site halfway down Loch Ness-side and yet another that looks as though it could be on the edge of Inverness itself. Then there are two old records previous to 1959 for the middle of Sutherland and near Cape Wrath in the north-west tip of the Highlands. Then, intriguingly, a book written by Harvie-Brown and Buckley at the end of the last century mentions a few sites near Loch Assynt and not far away a loch site near Lochinver. The paucity of records may indicate that the great crested newt is indeed very localised and rare in the Highlands but could it be that a lack of people looking for them is the real reason and with the recent records are there too many sites for it still to be classed as an introduction? We shall perhaps never know the answer but I for one will be very keen on looking for more sites this coming summer. Apart from looking in the water, turning over stones on the side of water bodies seems to be the answer, although these must be returned to the exact position as other animals will be living under them and of course under existing legislation the newts must not be handled or disturbed.

The suggestion that I might help in a black-throated diver survey was accepted with some pleasure but as I drove to the loch in question it was with the sobering thought that I cannot reveal to the reader where the loch lies as there are still egg collectors who could take advantage of that information. As we walked down through the woodland there was sufficient breeze to lower the impact of the dreaded Highland midge whilst in the heather-clad more open areas we found freshly emerged small pearl-bordered fritillary butterflies along with small heath and the first common blue of the year for us. Other insects included dragonflies: the common blue damselfly, the large red damselfly and the spectacular golden ringed dragonfly. On the slope leading down to the boat there were no fewer than five species of orchids: the fragrant which I bent over to catch that irresistible scent, the lesser butterfly, the heath-spotted, the northern marsh and the early marsh.

The weather was ideal for the survey with sunshine and only a slight ripple on the loch so that we were unlikely to miss any divers present. It was a large loch with some islands and a typical haunt of black-throated divers; five nest sites were known although even in the best of years only three are occupied. As we reached the first site on a small islet in a sheltered bay we saw two adults on the water and had magnificent views of these birds that so typify the wildness of the Highlands. The very brief search of the islet was discouraging as there was no sign of even an attempt at a nest scrape but at least we had seen a pair of birds. The next site was where a few years ago an otter had taken one of the adult divers off the nest and the other bird came back each summer on its own for three years. The other three sites were equally disappointing and there was not that same buoyancy in our step as we retraced our route up through the birch woodland.

In a glen off the main strath as I stood just below the snow line I watched an adult and an immature golden eagle soaring above me with broad wings effortlessly taking them higher and higher until they drifted over a high ridge and out of sight. A few minutes later I saw a male merlin with its blue-grey upper parts conspicuous as it turned in flight with the fluttering wings of its display, no doubt to a female I could not see. These were exciting views but what made the day for me was an incident with a much commoner species and as often happens with wildlife I came upon it by sheer chance. I had seen very many red deer carcases in the strath and the glen with many calves but also a scattering of hinds and stags. In one place where the burn was lined with old juniper scrub I saw a dead stag with its antlers half twisted under its body lying at the edge of the water as though it had been carried down some distance by the water. I walked over to the carcase to take a photograph thinking at the same time what effect this natural mortality would have on the over-population of red deer in some parts of the Highlands. I was later to learn from the estate stalker that most of the deaths had occurred early in the new year when the wind and rain had taken their toll. For the Highlands it had not been a bad winter but the problem was that the red deer were in a very poor condition at the onset of winter.

Then, re-crossing a tiny watercourse, I spotted a very large common lizard basking in the weak sunshine on a layer of moss close to the water's edge. I moved slightly and the lizard darted into the water where it remained submerged with its head about an inch below the surface. The water was so clear that I watched it for several minutes and took photographs as just occasionally its head would break the surface of the water to breathe. Apart from the eagles and merlin I saw mountain hares – still in their winter coats.

A few days at home gave me the opportunity of solving a wildlife mystery associated with the bird table which we now stock with appropriate food all the year round. Under the large bird table are four containers of peanuts and three of them empty in three days under the seemingly constant attention of siskins, chaffinches, greenfinches and three species of tits. The fourth container takes just over a day to empty and after watching the bird table I realised a male great spotted woodpecker was the reason, but the mystery was why it only goes for that one container of peanuts. The answer did not come easily until I noticed that the bottoms of the containers were all at different heights from the large stone under them. Only one container was in the right position for the woodpecker to use its stiff tail feathers on the stone to help support it as it hung from the container of peanuts. Another interesting observation was that when the woodpecker had finished it would drop to the stone below and gather up a beakful of small pieces of peanuts it had scattered and then it was off – no doubt feeding the pieces to the female in the nest hole which we suspect is in an oak at the far end of the paddock.

As if this was not delightful enough there had been an equally attractively coloured bird in the form of a drake mandarin duck that loafs around the edge of the larger of our three garden ponds. His close attention to the pond is because the female mandarin is incubating eggs in a nestbox only a few yards from the pond. In contrast, early one morning I watched a male redstart take a caterpillar into a nestbox where the female is incubating eggs. Despite these interesting records all the other small nestboxes in the garden are completely empty as in the spring all the resident tits – and siskins – were taken by two sparrow-hawks. The peanuts and the lower part of the bird table are now enmeshed with 2 in (5 cm) hole wire and this has made the sparrow-hawks go elsewhere. I know my attitude is not logical!

The main purpose of our trip to the dunes near Nairn was to search for small blue butterflies and we had some strange looks from people in the caravan site as butterfly nets were brandished. We were of course not collecting but merely using the nets to illustrate points to others in the group. The main problem with the visit was the strong winds although the sunshine meant that in sheltered places we should find butterflies on the wing. In the first sheltered area we found masses of kidney vetch on which the caterpillars of the small blue feed. Adult butterflies will take nectar from this plant and also bird's-foot trefoil of which there was plenty nearby. It was a few minutes before we spotted the first small blue: a female exploring the flowering head of a kidney vetch. The next specimen was a male with that hint of blue on the inside edge of the top of the wings. Small blues are unusual butterflies as they can exist in very small discrete colonies with sometimes fewer than 100 kidney vetch plants in flower.

Butterfly numbers in general on the dunes were not high, although no doubt because of the winds many were just sitting still and went unnoticed. In two hours we recorded six species including the small blue. The others were a single small copper, several dingy skippers, one small white, several small heaths and two meadow browns. The wild flowers were a riot of colour at every turn and the roses – especially the burnet rose – were at their best. Willow warblers were singing from the tops of the trees bordering the dunes whilst over some of the larger glades amongst the broom bushes skylarks were endlessly singing. However what made the day for me was when someone found a single egg of a small blue amidst the blossoms on a kidney vetch. It was barely visible to the naked eye but someone had a hand lens with them and it was almost awesome to look at such a tiny egg – the size of a small pin head – and think it would turn into a butterfly similar to those fluttering nearby.

Fortunately these days very few people collect butterflies, although some people still collect the chequered skippers from down near Fort William. People are more interested in making a collection of photographs and it is quite a challenge to try to cover every species in Britain. One of the most difficult ones to photograph must be the chequered skipper, as choosing the right day with the Highlands' variable weather can be a serious problem. Even if you stay in Fort William, by the time you have reached even the nearest sites the weather can have changed.

We also now know a great deal more about the distribution of butterflies in the Highlands largely due to the activities of the Highland Biological Recording Group and the enthusiasm of one individual who has co-ordinated everything. Some of the butterflies are difficult to find such as the small blue we searched for at Nairn. The mountain ringlet is even more difficult to locate, as is the northern brown argus that may often be overlooked as it flies over warm northern hillsides. There are a few areas that are managed with butterflies in mind, especially the important chequered skipper sites, but elsewhere management is often carrried out for other wildlife conservation reasons although these may well be compatible to butterfly requirements. The same can be said of other insects such as dragonflies. However we still need to know far more about the distribution of butterflies in the Highlands and their management requirements.

Kneeling on the shell beach looking for cowrie shells was tantalising as I had to face inland because of the angle of the sun, which meant that all the sea birds were behind me. It soon became obvious that a lot of cowries had been collected since my last visit three years before as it was some time before I found the first one. In half an hour I found only 20 cowries whereas over ten years ago I collected well over 300 in the same time. Most of the cowries were the northern species without spots and looking like very fine porcelain but four had the dark spots of the European cowrie.

I then went back to the car and used a telescope on the window mount to do a sea watch over an area of sea that according to the Ordnance Survey map is called the 'Boars of Duncansby'. The word Duncansby probably comes from the nearby Duncansby Head but I have failed to find the origin of the word 'Boars'. The only birds close in were several eiders with both males and females resting on the water. Over the sea was a constant stream of terns and kittiwakes but further out there were even more birds. Some of the auks were close enough to identify as puffins but in most cases the hundreds of birds flying past were simply noted down as 'auks'. Some gannets were flying to the east and others to the west and one of them was harried so relentlessly by a great skua that it disgorged its last meal. Then close in four sandwich terns flew past calling and occasionally dropping to the sea for tiny fish whilst a single black guillemot flew in and landed in front of me and immediately started diving for food.

On the way back the new Caithness Glass complex was visited and amongst the very large display of glass paperweights there was one with, inside, a miniature black bat in a flying position whilst above it was a tiny black spider hanging from a silk-like black thread. Unfortunately this exquisite piece was by far the most expensive paperweight so it stayed there!

In the 33 years that I have been working in wildlife conservation there have been times when there has been a feeling of optimism for the present and future. Reintroductions of such birds as the sea eagle and red kite have been successful, deciduous and Scots pine woodland is slowly spreading and more and more sites are being designated under legislation to protect wildlife. Just occasionally, however, incidents take place such as irresponsible and random poisoning that make me wonder just how much progress is being made. Last weekend there was one such incident on an estate near Inverness and I learnt the details through a friend. He and his wife had been out walking on a popular Highland walk through the hills when their labrador wandered off the path although still under control. Twenty yards (18 m) away the dog suddenly started yelping; my friend went to see what was happening and was staggered to find the dog trapped in a gin trap. This trap – illegal since 1973 in Scotland although much earlier in England – was well set, being attached to a large rock under peat, and just below the surface, with only the jagged jaws exposed so that it could not be seen. The bait? Freshly dead lambs round the trap no doubt intended to catch foxes. Fortunately the dog was only caught by the extreme end of its paw and was none the worse for the mishap. My friend contacted local conservationists who uplifted the trap the following day and delivered it to the nearest police station. The reason this trap was made illegal is that it is one of the most barbaric kinds; its victims could be fox, badger, red kite, golden eagle or buzzard as the trap is entirely non-selective and the birds or mammals suffer great pain. The trap was a mere 20 yards (18 m) from a well-used walkers' route from where children could have wandered but presumably the person who set the trap ignored all these possibilities, believing themselves above the present and past laws. I wonder why?

In west Sutherland Loch Assynt stretched away to the west from the limestone slopes and cliffs. Stronchrubie Cliff – house martins used to nest on the cliff – seemed to brood over Ardvreck Castle where at one time Charles St John – and others – plundered the nests of ospreys, either taking the eggs for collections or shooting the adult birds for mounting. On the lochside a pair of pied wagtails were gathering insects and taking them to chicks in a nest on a low cliff face. The pair of oystercatchers were at the water's edge and both fast asleep so it seemed likely that they had not been successful in rearing any young this year. Two hooded crows were mobbing a passing buzzard that seemed to be heading for a tree-covered cliff-site nest that I had photographed from a hide 25 years ago.

The most dramatic flowers amongst the species–rich grassland was one of the smallest as I had never seen such dense flower heads of the common milkwort. The rich blue flowers were not of the usual spreading prostrate form but were in tufts of dozens of small stems. Nearby the early purple orchids were at their best, indicating the lateness of the seasons this year, while the heath-spotted orchid was just beginning to open its flowers. In contrast the mountain avens were nearly all past their best although there were still a few creamy flowers to be seen. We headed for the wet flushes where the golden saxifrages cascaded down the edge of the splash zone of a waterfall. I am not very good at identifying lady's mantles and once past the common and the alpine lady's mantle I am lost, but even I could tell there was a rarer lady's mantle present. Sheep had been taken off this area a few years ago and it was disconcerting to see the number of small birch trees coming in that could swamp the flower-rich areas. Conservationists had welcomed the removal of the sheep but it is not that simple as some of them may have to be brought back for controlled grazing to perpetuate the rich flora.

The lady on the telephone sounded very concerned, as the small factory she worked in near Inverness had been invaded by frogs. She said there were frogs in the buildings, frogs sitting around in the car park whilst others had fallen into two drains where one or two had died. As I did not know the site I went out to see for myself and give what advice I could and I was soon driving into the car park. A temporary cardboard sign simply said BEWARE/FROGS and there was the young lady busy picking them up. As it turned out they were all toads but the same problem remained as a pair with the male on top of the female walked under my vehicle. We rescued as many as we could and put them in the nearby pond where some of their companions were croaking away. My first advice was temporarily to cover the two drains to stop more falling in whilst we looked around.

What had happened was that the new factory and car park had been built on ground between where the toads hibernated for the winter and their spring breeding site – the pond on the other side of the complex. The drains would be the first priority, with dead and living toads – along with a few live palmate newts – to be taken out and then fine mesh grille put over the drains to stop access but to allow rainwater to flow through. Elsewhere a bucket with a small amount of water could be used frequently to catch the toads which should then be placed carefully into the pond. I stressed the need to use gloves, as the secretion from a handled toad can cause problems. We then looked at the pond where there were at least 50 clumps of frogs spawn so at least 50 females were in that breeding colony. The small pond – about 20 yards (18 m) across – is one of the few places in the Highlands where frogs, toads and newts breed in the same place. What made the visit for me, however, was the enthusiasm and concern of the young lady and as I left she was about to change the sign to BEWARE/TOADS.

If anyone thinks television or filming is glamorous then they should have been with me earlier in June when I went 100 miles (160 km) south of Inverness to help in a BBC television film about chequered skipper butterflies. It was raining when I arrived, that fine Highland rain that eventually penetrates everywhere despite waterproofs, and of course the midges were out in force. The producer, sound recorder, cameraman and assistant cameraman were waiting for me and after inspecting the site for filming we spent the next two hours waiting for the rain to cease; it did not. The wait was pleasantly interrupted by the sight of a pine marten running through a woodland glade and this seemed to galvanise us into action.

The camera was set up so that I could walk along a woodland ride towards the camera with a net in my hand looking for butterflies. This seemed slightly incongruous in the rain but one or two brimstone moths did fly up from the grass as I walked through it. There were consolations because all the time we were filming a wood warbler and tree pipit were singing away despite the rain. The first take, I was told, was perfect – but I had been walking too fast. On the second take I tripped over a tree root and on the third I was still too fast. Then it was close-up time with me talking about food plants of butterflies and caterpillars, how the caterpillar coped with the grass blade it would feed on and what management was involved. By this time I was soaked and the midges were annoying and I found as the afternoon wore on that I was having difficulty in keeping up with the amusing banter between the four people. I had also been 'wired up' for sound so that even from a distance anything I said could be heard by the sound recorder. I found the whole experience very tiring possibly because of the weather conditions but mainly because I found it difficult to keep up mentally with four very professional people. I just hope I never see the film, which should be called *Butterflies in the Rain*.

It was about three years ago when I gave advice for rabbit control on this dune system on the west coast of Sutherland. In mid June this year I had the chance to revisit the site and see if the flora on the rich machair had been saved. The main problems causing the severe erosion were a combination of rabbits, wind and rain and the results were extensive areas of mobile sand. So mobile was the sand that it frequently entered the nearby croft houses and when it was windy there was little point in putting washing out on the lines in the garden. Several methods to control the sand were tried such as fences, laying down brush, planting marram grass and using polythene. However, in the end, whilst some areas were restored, the best method was putting down a layer of wet peat. There are still some areas of open sand to be dealt with but it was good to see very large areas of herb-rich machair. Deep purple northern marsh orchids contrasted with the yellow of buttercup and bird's-foot trefoil, the blue and violet of the large wild pansies and the striking white colour of daisies.

I headed for the shell midden on the side of one of the sand dunes but I never did reach it as trotting over the shells were the chicks of a pair of ringed plovers. One of the adults gave a classic display of injury feigning as she staggered over the ground with one wing trailing as if injured. I am sure it would have fooled any predator but I backed off so there was no need for the bird to continue with the remarkable display. I stood on a cliff overlooking the sea and marine islands such as Handa to the south whilst inland were the impressive hills of Canisp and Suilven. Fulmars glided effortlessly past me and so close I felt I could have reached out and touched them, whilst to my right arctic terns were feeding. At my feet were the pink blossoms of sea pinks, thyme blossoms were just opening and I crushed a leaf between my fingers. The wildness of the Highlands!

The herd of whooper swans were grazing on a field just inland from this small east coast village in the Highlands. There were 57 adults but only seven juveniles, indicating a poor breeding season last year in their home ground of Iceland.

The very first bird I looked at had rings on its legs – a yellow plastic ring on one leg and a metal one on the other. Once in the past I have managed to read the numbers and letters on a yellow leg ring through the telescope but this bird was much too far away. I could have tried to get closer but the birds were very wary and this was likely to be their last feeding ground before flying north and I did not wish to risk disturbing them. However as I was scanning the birds I suddenly found that two of them had yellow neck rings and as these have larger numbers and letters the telescope might reveal some secrets. With the telescope on the window mount I focused and found it fairly easy to read the numbers and letters. One was 2F49 and the other 2J66, although there was the possibility that the 2 could have been a Z.

Then it was on to Rockfield for an even bigger surprise as amongst the fulmars flying past there was a darker bird that turned out to be the much rarer so-called 'blue phase' fulmar. This is a darker colour form of fulmar that is commoner in the high arctic colonies and as an indication of its rarity I have only ever seen three before. One was in south-east Iceland, one on St Kilda and one on North Rona. When I did get back to the telephone the Wildfowl and Wetlands Trust at Slimbridge informed me that the two neck rings had been put on the swans in eastern Iceland in 1994 by a group of ringers from Denmark. A letter has gone to the ringers concerned so that I can get more details, especially as the neck rings could have been read elsewhere in the birds' travels. How interesting that the airmail letter to Denmark was only 25p!

Many thanks to those readers of this Country Diary who wrote or telephoned me about the ice houses they know of in the Highlands. These contacts have added several more ice houses to the ever growing list that now numbers 45, although I estimate that the final list will be twice that number.

One reader remembered two ice houses at Culkein near Lochinver in Sutherland on the east coast and she recalls the ice being carried by horse and cart from Lochinver where presumably it had been taken by boat. The ice houses were used to store salmon that were fished from the bay in summer although the practice seems to have stopped during the war and started again in the fifties when one of the ice houses was used as a cold store, although ice does not appear to have been used then. Another source of information may well be Ordnance Survey maps as I have been informed that whilst ice houses are not normally shown on the 1:50,000 they will be on the 1:25,000 but that still means a very large number of maps to look at!

As regards the planned inventory I took out the first recording forms two weeks ago – an excuse to drive up the east coast to Littleferry near Golspie. Fortunately the ice house here is a listed building so there was at least some information from the Archaeological Department. This was perhaps just as well as I did not know how to describe the unusual shape of the structure which I am assured is a cuspate foreland, so it looks as if I will have to get used to a terminology that is new to me. On the way back I looked briefly at the large ice house on the side of the road at Bonar Bridge, which would no doubt have been used by the local salmon fishing station. As for the ice house reported at the Meikle Ferry near Dornoch, I simply could not find it so it may well have been demolished, unless it was tucked away out of sight.

Taking nine of the older pupils from Farr Primary School on a 'wildlife drive' was daunting to say the least but it turned out to be very enjoyable and I was surprised just how much they knew about the countryside and its wildlife. For example I was told it was a mountain hare even as the animal sat and posed for us before lolloping off and showing just how long its rear legs were compared with the front pair. The red deer stags were so close to the vehicle that the velvet on the antlers was clearly seen and two of them rose on their back legs and boxed, much to the delight of the children who all said it was the closest they had ever been to a red deer. The wild goats were in two separated groups with nannies and their delightful kids in one part of the strath whilst further east were the billies including one we estimated at eight years old by counting the annual growth rings on the horns. As the rain stopped, a party of sika deer, hinds and calves, came out from the shelter of the trees to graze on open grassland affording us excellent views of this introduced species that looked very dark compared with the red deer.

On the way back we stopped to look at a dipper's nest under a bridge over a burn and I had forgotten just how excited youngsters could get despite the fact that we did not see the dipper itself. Yes, the pupils knew all about the burning of strips of heather for the red grouse and they knew the bird was a buzzard as it drifted along the edge of a wood. I had left two antlers at the school for the pupils to look at and discuss when we returned, one of them being the short antlers of a roe deer and the other a cast antler of a red deer I had picked up in the strath earlier this year. I left each pupil with a large black and white photograph of a red deer stag partly to remind them of the day and partly because I enjoyed myself so much. The drive will become an annual event!

Red Fox

Summer

At the small Coire Loch in this glen most of the dragonflies are on the wane although the Highland darter and the black darter are still coming into their own with immature golden wings flashing in the sunlight. Every step through the rank heather surrounding the loch disturbs one or two darters that with fragile wings try to fly away. At the edge of the water on a reed stem a darter is just emerging at mid afternoon and in half an hour has creamy wings extended but looking so obvious and vulnerable to predators. Green lestes damselflies are also plentiful and active in the sunlight that has been so lacking this Highland summer.

But there are many other things to see in this important and rich fragment of the old Caledonian pine forest. Buzzards mew overhead – they bred in the top of an isolated pine – whilst the success of the crossbills this year is indicated by the frequency of parties flying over. Am I right in thinking that crossbills breeding in our Highland pine forests are the supposed endemic Scottish crossbill? Droppings on a woodland path reveal the presence of capercaillie but there is no sign of the black grouse although I know they are there. For years the pine marten had disappeared from these forests but in the last decade it has spread and apparently increased despite continual persecution – both accidental and otherwise. One way to see them these days is to wait at dusk near a full litter bin where they often scavenge, but I was more than content to see their spraints marking territory at three places at the loch margin. Wildcats are more difficult to see but they haunt Glen Affric along with badger, roe deer and red deer. I could easily have spent the whole day at the Coire Loch as it is buffeted from the great dark green pines by a sphagnum bog, where the sundews trap tiny insects.

Most of my sightings of sparrow-hawks in our garden have been during the winter when the bird table attracts a variety of species including siskins. The sparrow-hawk will either circle above the house and suddenly rush down or – as I saw once, early in the morning – it will fly slowly up the road about 10 ft (3 m) off the ground searching for an unwary bird. At one time – when the kills in the garden included greenfinches and siskins – I debated in my mind the ethics of attracting birds to a garden where a sparrow-hawk regularly hunted but I came to no conclusion.

In mid August this year I was near one of the garden ponds and was vaguely conscious of the house sparrows chattering away in the thorn bush tight against the side of the garage when suddenly I heard a rush of wings. As I turned to look there was the briefest view of a sparrow-hawk going into the bush not 10 yds (9 m) from me. The sparrows scattered in all directions and for a moment there was an uneasy silence and then a noisy clattering of wings within the dense foliage. I presumed the sparrow-hawk was dealing with its prey but as the noise continued I began to realise that something was wrong. Reaching the bush I hesitantly parted some of the twigs and there, only 2 ft (0.6 m) from me, was an adult female sparrow-hawk. The noise I had heardwas her wings clattering at the window glass of the garage as she tried to get through the glass to escape the bush.

Left on her own it was possible the bird would injure herself so I reached into the bush and clasped the bird from the side. It is difficult to describe the feeling of having such a bird in the hand but after admiring the long yellow legs and strong-looking bill I released her. The bird soared round the house three times before drifting across to the open fields. I was left wondering whether she would be back this winter – after the greenfinches and siskins.

Behind the low dunes a small field was 'fenced' with lichen-covered Caithness flagstones and the short grass held scattered groups of lapwings, starlings and rock doves. The rock doves all looked pure and as they rose their white rumps flashed clearly. True rock doves are now scarce, as hybrids with feral pigeons are commonplace; perhaps only these northern coastlines and the Western Isles still support the true strain.

In the tall uncut grass of the field margin there was a blaze of colour as ragged robin competed with corn marigold and I wondered if any corncrakes had bred earlier. Last year I heard a single male calling from a small lochan a few miles to the west, although as usual it was difficult to prove whether it was breeding. Hopefully the two corn buntings that sat on a flagstone had bred as even up here the numbers of these plump buntings have decreased in the last ten years. Out to sea birds seemed everywhere including gannets in small groups heading – for some reason – north, or single gannets feeding by their spectacular dives that sent up cascades of spray as they hit the water. Fulmars skimmed the quiet sea or wheeled endlessly round the distant sheer cliffs of Duncansby Head whilst the great skuas harried the passing kittiwakes and gulls.

But I was more interested in the shoreline as I just could not believe the vast quantity of shells, dazzling to the eye in the bright sunshine. Perhaps the most impressive were the large whelk shells. In some places they dominated large areas and in layers of about 10 in (25 cm) deep under which an array of other shells could be found. One of the Scottish names for my favourite shell – the cowrie – is 'groat' and I just had to find one but it was not difficult and I soon had examples of both the European and northern cowrie. It did not surprise me to learn later that cowries have long been sought here and at one time necklaces made from cowries were sold locally.

From the air one could be forgiven for thinking that the Uists and Benbecula consisted solely of water, bare rock and peat with associated peat cuttings criss-crossing the flat landscape. But driving along the narrow roads – how delightful that everyone waves and uses passing places correctly – there are variations. The cut cornfields are covered with real stooks, occasionally with pure rock doves feeding on top of them, whilst the machair supports flocks of lapwings and golden plovers. Wildfowl seem everywhere and there are so many mute swans it is difficult to believe that these came from a deliberate introduction late last century. My destination was Loch Druidibeg National Nature Reserve where I was to meet up with a task party from the Scottish Conservation Project Trust.

This group of 11 young people was replacing a deer fence round the small plantation. The first group of four I met were engrossed in straining line wire to a massive straining post which was surprisingly solid in such a depth of peat. Fortunately it was sunny for my visit but the wind was annoying as it swept across the open landscape and created turmoil on the large loch nearby. I walked the fence with the trust's field officer, Keith Wilson, and we discussed the progress of the fence and the plans for next year. Then it was back to the trust's vehicles and lunch à la trust style. It was clearly a happy, energetic group, mainly due to the infectious enthusiasm of the task leader, Gail Churchill, who led all the tasks at Beinn Eighe in Wester Ross this year that had culminated in the reopening of the unique mountain trail for the public. Driving back along the machair it was refreshing to think of the group of young people and their 'conservation in action' activities.

More information about the wide range of wildlife conservation tasks by the SCPT can be obtained from: Balallan House, 24 Allan Park, Stirling FK8 2QG.

Single rifle shots in the morning echo across the strath and the hills around. They indicate that the red deer stag cull is yet again under way and many estates must have breathed a sigh of relief. Last winter the game dealers' price for venison dropped dramatically from 80p per pound to as little as 40p per pound. The reason was the collapse of the venison market in Continental Europe, particularly Germany which takes around 70% of Scottish venison. This was partly because large amounts of venison from New Zealand had flooded the market and partly because radiation levels of Scottish venison, after the Chernobyl disaster, were unacceptable on the European market. This very low venison price meant that it was not economical to run estates based mainly as deer forests and it could possibly have led to mandatory culls or even leaving shot carcases on the hill. So it was with bated breath that we awaited the prices from the game merchants. Fortunately the prices have risen to around 78p per pound.

However the market is still shaky and the crisis point will again be the hind prices later in the year which could lead to serious long-term consequences for the Highlands. Low prices would mean yet more cuts in estate staff with the result that the red deer population would rise yet again. It has been estimated that the Scottish Highlands will support around 150,000 red deer, but recent estimates suggest the actual population may be around 300,000. Although now found on areas unknown to support deer in living memory there are increasing areas denied to them by afforestation. The result is a gradual run-down in the general condition of red deer and high mortality even in moderate winters. Let us hope that the venison prices can be maintained, for the future of red deer and the deer forests of the Highlands. Whatever one thinks about the culling of red deer, the market has a major effect on the Highlands' economy.

On 10 August a combination of planes, helicopters, boats and yachts brought 50 of us to the church on Hirta for the final stage in the World Heritage listing of this National Nature Reserve. We had gathered to mark the unveiling of a plaque that signifies the new status of the archipelago under UNESCO, the first natural site to be so listed in Britain and the first site ever in Scotland. It seemed fitting that the plaque should be hung on an inside wall of the church as in the past this building had been a sanctuary to the original St Kildans. It was a simple but moving ceremony with the speakers talking about the cultural and architectural interests apart from the importance of the fauna, the latter including a million breeding sea birds.

Afterwards we broke up into small groups to explore the village and particularly the main street and the houses where once lived a bird-culture based community eating the eggs and flesh of puffins and gannets and, perhaps the most important species, because of its oil, the fulmar. In 1977 over 44,000 pairs nested but the latest count indicates 63,000 pairs. The fulmars have also spread and this was indicated by the pairs we saw on top of the cleitean as these have only been colonised in the last few years. These birds launched themselves from the cleitean and at head height swept round us with stiff-backed wings as if inquisitive at the intrusion. As it was August many of the sea birds had left the islands but when the helicopter took us round Soay and then Boreray and the Stacs there was an abundance of fulmars and gannets.

As we left I carried with me a number of lasting impressions but they were dominated by two. The first was the singing of Psalm 121 in the church, as if momentarily the village had come alive again, and the second was Stac Lee with its gannets. It was well described some years ago by the first Director-General of UNESCO, Sir Julian Huxley, as the 'most majestic sea rock in existence'.

After having led several expeditions to Iceland it has enabled me to look on the Scottish Highlands as a landform shaped by the great glaciers and to imagine how certain formations have taken place. So I was looking forward to the initiative of the Forestry Commission in interpreting the effect of glacial rivers over the Struie about 30 miles (48 km) north of Inverness. Whilst the workmen were constructing the car park they suddenly realised that a pair of hen harriers had a nest on the side of the valley just below the site and were easily observed. Rather than postpone the glacial project, the Forestry Commission took a bold move and erected screening either side of a Portakabin hide, and the travelling public were invited in once the eggs had hatched to view the young in the nest. I was invited to visit the hide to try and photograph the chicks and was met by a very enthusiastic trainee forester with several pairs of binoculars available for visitors and a telescope permanently focused on the nest. A notice-board outside the hide gave the latest information and indicated that during the morning meadow pipits had been brought in as food by the female and it was fascinating to see the active chicks.

It was only ten days later that once again I was out on Forestry Commission ground in the same area but this time looking for capercaillie. A roe deer was feeding in the Drovers Stance – a field used by the old drovers to keep their cattle overnight – and a young buzzard called from some old pines above me. Along the ride side clumps of stagshorn clubmoss had pale fruiting bodies 6 in (15 cm) high and everywhere there were masses of cross-leaved heath and bell heather – a sign of how rapidly the year is passing. As it happened I was not to see any 'capers', although judging by the number of droppings they were certainly present. What made the day for me was the first painted lady butterfly fluttering along the ride; was it a migrant or had it just hatched?

This deer farm park lies a few miles west of Inverness and has a wide variety of animals and birds including rare sheep, poultry and goat breeds along with red, fallow and roe deer. The day we went there were few people despite the sunshine but it gave us the opportunity to photograph various species without having people moving them around. We were particularly interested in the sheep as they included not only Soay sheep that we know from St Kilda but, as a separate breed, the Boreray sheep. According to the catalogue they are not as old as some other island breeds as they are from the late nineteenth century when Soay sheep were crossed with Scottish Blackface. Next time I go to St Kilda and circle the island of Boreray I will perhaps look at the sheep in a different frame of mind, as with Blackface in their blood I had never believed them to be a rare breed.

Although I often see red deer calves on the hill I was still fascinated by being so close to them; they were in an open paddock through which the visitors just wandered and the hinds and calves showed no sign of fear. In contrast the stags were well fenced in and viewed from a greater distance but the beasts were lying down in long bracken although their heads and huge velvet-covered antlers could easily be seen as they flicked their ears against the flies. The 'wild' goats were also in an open paddock but they kept their distance, with one old billy looking very dominant as it strode around. Then there were Tamworth pigs, Saanen and Toggenburg goats, Dexter cattle, a magnificent Longhorn cow, a Welsummer cockerel, shelduck, mallard and a variety of rabbits. The success of such ventures is often dubious but this farm park worked because of the spacious layout that still enabled close views to be obtained and the fact that it was very clean indeed. The visit also gave us the chance to visit the Wagnerian-looking hydro scheme building across the road and to count 48 occupied house martin nests.

In the sun-filled glade around me a golden ringed dragonfly was stalking insects as its circular route took it amidst the Scots pine branches. The black and gold markings of the dragonfly were bright in the sunlight and I saw it take several tiny insects that I hoped were all midges as they were on the warpath with the usual severity of the Scottish Highlands. Beinn Eighe – pronounced 'ben-ay' – lies in Ross-shire and its 12,000 acres (4800 ha) was the first National Nature Reserve in Britain. I was on but a very small part of it as I walked the Glas Leitire – Gaelic for the grey slopes – nature trail that spiralled about 1 mile (1.6 km) through a combination of old pine, young birch and heather. There was not that much wildlife to be seen as it was the wrong time of day, with a few people around, but the number of pine marten droppings gave an indication they were there. The birds included a wren that might well have followed me all round the trail, a buzzard that two people were convinced was a golden eagle and a male redstart that crossed the path in front of me.

But throughout the walk it was the views of Loch Maree that thrilled the eye as it was dead calm and I could clearly make out three fishing boats down at the east end of the loch where the grey-lag geese breed. During the walk splashes of colour in the vegetation came in the form of bell heather and cross-leaved heath as the heather as such was only just breaking through into blossom. The trail leaflet mentions sundews in two places but these went some time ago as people took them away in the mistaken belief that they can grow them in their gardens. Attempts at transplanting other sundews have met with the same result so when the leaflet is rewritten any reference to these insectivorous plants will unfortunately be left out. The self-guiding trail has 12 stopping points marked by numbers on cairns and the leaflet describes a range of aspects from soil profiles to fungi and deer damage to trees.

The Twin Otter took us from Stornoway to Benbecula in a storm that made us fly at only 500 ft (152 m) over an angry sea that was dotted with flying fulmars and gannets, with the latter adults conspicuous against the dark water but as white as the turbulent foam off the tops of the waves. After a surprisingly gentle landing I was soon heading down the west coast of South Uist where for a while the sun was threatening to break through. July must be one of the best months to see birds in the Western Isles and it was with some difficulty that apart from two stops to watch birds I forced myself to reach my destination. The first stop was a bay just south of the airport where on the seaweed mixed parties of starlings and turnstones were feeding. There are so many starlings in the Highlands now that it is hard to believe that around 1800 it was probably extinct in Scotland except in Shetland and the Outer Hebrides. Where these small populations survived they are now recognised as a separate species, *Sturnus vulgaris zetlandicus,* and these were the birds I could see with the turnstones. In the bay were eider and all were busy diving for food while the ever-attentive gulls sat nearby waiting for any scraps.

The second stop was for a few minutes in a long and wide passing place where I watched a bunch of greylag geese flying from a loch over the nearby machair and with the wind increasing they were having difficulty in holding their course. Later in the day I stood in a field where sheaves formed stooks that in turn formed stacks and there seemed to be birds everywhere as I sheltered behind a large stack. On the nearby loch were mute swans and their cygnets, dozens of mallard and teal and a pair of gadwall that rose as I watched and crossed to another loch.The rain was now horizontal but there was no time to think about it as a flock of 50 rock doves descended on the field and then nine large birds whose wing bars gave them away as black-tailed godwits.

For over 100 miles (160 km) of the journey from Inverness to the north coast of Caithness we were driving through a haar of sea mist that stretched a few miles inland. Visibility in most places was restricted to 50 yds (46 m) which made for frustrating driving, but for my companion it was much worse as he had never been to Caithness before, and would have liked to have seen more of the scenery. Just before Thurso we went into sunshine and a few miles further on we were on the dune links of the Dunnet Links National Nature Reserve. The object of the visit was to discuss management of the mainly 1956 plantings of exotic conifers planted by the Forestry Commission that were interspersed with open areas of grassland supporting a rich fauna and flora.

It was difficult to concentrate on the complex and far-reaching management issues as in the sunshine the small blue, dark green fritillary and hundreds of common blue butterflies were on the wing along with others such as the meadow brown and the unusual northern form of the large heath which have no spots on their under-wings. The small fire pond, now square but soon to be extended with scalloped margins, contained scores of tadpoles and a few of last year's toads and frogs on the margins. The bogbean had gone to seed and on the leaves were resting three species of damselflies: the small red, the green lestes and the common blue. The nearby marshy area had clumps of ragged robin contrasting against the bright yellow of marsh marigold and whiteness of cotton grass. The main orchid was the dwarf purple, whose large flower heads were conspicuous as opposed to the greenness of the large twayblade and frog orchids. The discussions ranged from clear-felling failed crop Corsican pine to three stages of thinning and extending glades but then we found a few Scottish primroses in flower – the lilac pink flowers with the yellow eye as attractive as ever and out came the cameras.

Our recent drive through Sutherland left me with a variety of impressions, starting with the sudden change of colour as we slipped through Elphin north of Ullapool as there, suddenly, was the limestone landscape. The green vegetation stood out whether from the strips of crofters' fields or the grassland at the edge of the loch. A few miles further on Stronchrubie Cliff looked weathered as it overlooked Loch Assynt and the ruins of Ardvreck Castle where the osprey used to nest. The area of woodland that makes up Loch a' Mhuilinn National Nature Reserve faces out to a sprinkling of marine islands but the wood, soberingly, reminded us of what this part of the Sutherland landscape should be like if it had not been degraded by overburning and overgrazing.

Further north near Durness we looked out over the beautiful Balnakeil Bay and across to Faraidh Head where one of the few mainland puffin colonies can found. It was from this peninsula that red deer were once driven into the sea and chased by boats until they became exhausted and were taken for venison. I had wanted to walk the grassy coastline where Scottish primrose and frog orchids abound to get to some rocks where I knew a few cowrie shells could be found, one of my secret places to find my favourite shells. But it was not to be as since my last visit a golf course had appeared and with people teeing off towards me I gave up and returned to the car, disappointed and frustrated.

We turned east and watched fulmars gliding over the road at Smoo Cave and then we branched south to run along under the shore of Loch Hope under the 3040 ft (927 m) of Ben Hope towering above us. The red deer stags would soon be bellowing from the steep slopes but for now the cull was on and signs simply said NO WALK-ING OR CLIMBING presumably meaning everywhere! It was a day when we saw a juvenile black-throated diver on a loch.

North Rona

North Rona   *12 July 1990*

Over the years my efforts to reach some of the remote islands off the Scottish coast such as St Kilda, the Monach Isles, North Rona and Sula Sgeir have often been thwarted by the weather, whether the transport has been by boat or helicopter. Last Friday these thoughts were running through my mind as I sat in the Meteorological Office at Stornoway Airport literally waiting for a front to pass through before the ominous-looking Chinook helicopter could take off. Soon we were passing over the lighthouse at the Butt of Lewis and out over the open sea where I looked fruitlessly for whales and dolphins whilst we travelled the 46 miles (74 km) to the island of North Rona.

Then as if by magic carpet 35 minutes later we were touching down on my most favourite of islands to be greeted by the great skuas and great black-backed gulls. Within minutes we were walking through the territory of a pair of great skuas who were showing the usual aggression but this time not actually making contact as they swept within inches of our heads.

Heading to the southern aspect of the island we were soon amidst the remains of the village – the island was inhabited until the last family left in 1844 – and the burial ground where the headstones are few and very basic. The nearby St Ronan's cell is reputed to have been built by a hermit monk in the eighth or ninth century and may be the oldest Christian building in Britain that is in its original state. The attached small church is probably of medieval origin but would have been used by the last residents for worship. Incredibly, souvenir hunters have made their mark on such a remote island as North Rona as some of the crude cross-shaped headstones have disappeared and some of the kiln stones have also gone. We had three hours on the island and were thrilled by the grey seals, puffins, rock doves, great skuas – including a well-grown chick – and the juvenile kittiwakes learning to fly.

It could have been my companions with between us that gentle banter so characteristic of people very interested in wildlife. Or it could have been the fact that I was to be shown a new orchid – new to me at least. But whatever the reason it was a magical few hours on the west coast of Sutherland with the backcloth of the island-studded sea to the west and inland the high hills all touched by clouds. At our first stop we walked through some birch woodland and over a small bridge where there was a fresh pine marten dropping and further along the track some less fresh ones so it looked as if it was a well-used track. Out of the trees a small dusky-looking moth – a chimney sweeper – was fluttering amidst the tall grasses, whilst on the return walk in the same area we saw a pristine, freshly emerged dark green fritillary hanging from a grass stem and seemingly without a scale out of place. Our destination was the steep almost scree slopes where we found an abundance of plants with the speciality being hundreds of pyramidal bugle, many of them already gone to seed. Orchids were represented by butterfly, heath-spotted and fragrant orchids whilst there were two groups of tall, stately, melancholy thistles, perhaps so called because when used medicinally it was supposed to make people happy. There was plenty of movement amidst the plants as small, brown unidentified moths fluttered past, immature grasshoppers leapt around and young frogs jumped as only frogs can.

But this was not the place of the new orchid and later we approached a dangerous looking bog and started to scan the fringing sphagnum mosses and then it was there before me: a less than 2 in (5 cm) high bog orchid and the hairs on the back of my neck stiffened in excitement. We counted 14 spikes, some of them only about a quarter of an inch up from the mosses. We cautiously circled the bog but could find no other bog orchids.

Before we moved into our present old farmhouse in Strathnairn we had intended to retire to the Loch Sunart area west of Fort William in eight years' time. Such plans have now been mutually forgotten but it is still thrilling to visit the Sunart area and my last visit in mid September was no exception. The highlight of the day was to be shown a dark, wet, rocky outcrop on a north-facing slope with a cleft under a canopy of low birch and ash and there were both the Tunbridge filmy fern and the Wilson's filmy fern, growing side by side, which is a rare occurrence. Even I could see the toothed edge of what I call the 'leaves' of the Tunbridge filmy fern which is by far the rarest of the two species in the Highlands.

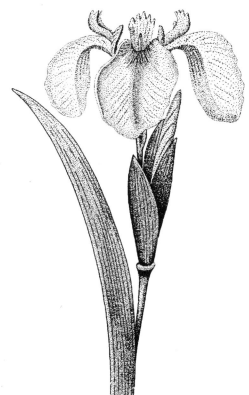

Yellow Flag

Although it was not sunny it was bright and there were a few courting pairs of speckled wood butterflies in the open glades; with such a high rainfall in this part of the Highlands it is fortunate that these butterflies can fly in quite dull weather. They were obviously attracted to the white roof of the van we were using although it was difficult to say if this was because of the warmth of the metal or the reflected bright light. Some species of dragonflies are readily attracted to white signs or the whitish bark of birch but I cannot recall butterflies doing this apart from small tortoiseshells on the white walls of our house. When we came out of the wood there were six speckled woods on top of the van roof with their wings fully extended and motionless and reluctant to move.

Whilst having lunch it was difficult to know where to look as a common seal was fishing in the sea loch, a party of 20-plus siskins were down on the ride almost at ground level taking seed from various plants, two ravens croaked overhead, a buzzard mewed over the woodland and there was a very active wood ant's nest a few yards away from our van. The view across the loch was outstanding as the sea was dead calm apart from small areas of disturbance close to the shore where whitebait were fleeing from predatory mackerel and I just wished I had a fishing rod to hand. The long drive back was through a landscape that was preparing for autumn and it seemed significant at home that the house martins had left for their long journey south.

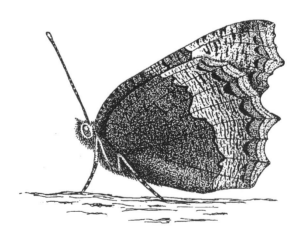

Tortoiseshell Butterfly

Having found only one source of modern corn dollies in the Highlands I had wrongly assumed that these intriguing straw models did not have a role in the old customs of the north. From a variety of sources it has been very interesting to find that there was so much variation in the use and meaning of corn dollies from district to district. Much of the old customs revolved round the belief that the whole cycle of harvest was controlled by the corn mother whilst the corn spirit carried on the success of the harvest from year to year. In most cases the corn spirit was believed to seek sanctuary in the last sheaf to be cut and this was clothed to resemble a corn maiden or dolly. This was kept through the winter months and then either planted in the first furrow to be ploughed in the next year or given to the horses before the ploughing started. Local custom varied considerably, as sometimes the first sheaf was thought to hold the corn spirit and this was kept until the following year. The treatment of the last of the harvest varied as sometimes instead of gathering the last sheaf they threw their scythes at the remains of the crop or sometimes simply trampled it down.

The smaller corn dollies that we know today were also made and in the Highlands they had a variety of uses from putting them on the ricks to stop witches landing on them to hanging one in a larder as it meant that the room would hold enough food for the family until the following harvest. There are many different corn dolly patterns with the older designs having a different meaning in the old customs, although each design meant the same thing throughout the Highlands and for that matter the Islands. The straw used had to be hollow and clean whether from rye, oats or, the most popular, wheat and in the Highlands the finest rye straw was used to make brooches using intricate knots. The custom at harvest time was for young lads to give these brooches to their sweethearts to wear.

The last time I had visited this famous landmark in the Highlands had been 20 years before so it was with some anticipation that I drove through the woodland to the osprey hide. Although it was overcast there were plenty of Scotch argus butterflies flying and there were so many that I had some difficulty in not hitting them with the car! Despite the efforts of the RSPB since the ospreys colonised this site in 1959, there have been problems such as egg collectors, gales and vandalism such as the main trunk of the tree holding the nest being cut off. Even the hides and display/shop building have suffered from mindless vandals who set fire to the complex last winter and razed it to the ground complete with all the shop's stock. Although the new structure is temporary it is very well laid out and there were several telescopes and binoculars for visitors to use. There were good views through the telescopes and reasonable views through my binoculars but I was not prepared for the marvellous innovation that had been installed three years ago.

There in the corner of the large hide was a television set showing live pictures complete with sound from the nest and as the camera was slightly higher than the nest the pictures were almost breathtaking, showing two well-feathered chicks. Even as we watched the camera was turned to focus attention on the female osprey that had landed in a nearby tree out of sight of the hide itself. We were told by an enthusiastic and knowledgeable RSPB warden that we were lucky to see the birds as they were the last ones to be fledged in Scotland as the pair had been late in settling down. Ironically this saved them from a fate experienced by older chicks that had died from the cold rain of early summer. The notice-board in the hide kept visitors informed of the latest happenings and it indicated that the larger chick had taken its first flight that morning on wings that will hopefully soon take it to Africa for the winter.

Telephone calls about wildlife vary considerably at this time of the year from someone who wanted to know what to do with a young bat that was crawling over the kitchen floor to someone who wanted to know what to do with a dead badger. Just occasionally there is a call with a difference and such was the case when a lady rang me to ask me to identify a small animal she had found in her garden as she did not know whether it was a newt or a lizard. The description made me leave immediately as it sounded like a great crested newt and the reason for my interest was that as far as I know there is only one place in the Highlands where these large newts occur and this is in a series of adjoining kettle holes. It was therefore with great anticipation that in a garden next to an old curling pond I turned over a stone to reveal a male and female great crested newt and, as is often the case over such thrilling moments, the hairs on the back of my neck were raised. I pointed out the diagnostic features such as the black skin with orange/red underparts, the warty-looking skin from which it is given its other name of warty newt, the size of them and finally the streak of silver on the tail of the male.

Under a stone in an adjoining garden there was another specimen on its own but it could not be sexed as the end of the tail was missing. This new colony is just over 7 miles (11 km) – as the newt walks – from the kettle holes colony and a night visit is called for next spring when a torch may reveal what sort of numbers are involved. As with the three known colonies of smooth newts in the Highlands the great crested newt colonies are almost certainly from escapes or introductions. Despite extensive searching in the last 15 years it still seems that the only native newt in the Highlands – and it is very widespread and abundant – is the palmate newt. One colony of palmate newts I studied on the island of Rum hibernated underwater, which is unusual.

Standing in the Visitor Centre at Knockan Cliff on the borders of Sutherland and Ross-shire my mind was taken back to 1970 when I attended the opening of the then very forward-looking centre. As warden of the National Nature Reserve I had to arrange the exhibits but because there was no money it was simply a case of putting up my own black and white photographs with captions. I well remember the trouble in producing the prints as the peaty water supply in the house where we lived at the opposite end of the reserve meant they all came out looking like the old sepia-tone prints. Now the small centre has both wildlife and geological displays of a very high standard and the only aspect common to both 1970 and today is the 'touch table' with various items such as an antler, the cocoon of an emperor moth, a shed snake skin and the skull of a badger.

Outside, a walk round the nature trail revealed that little had changed as far as the wildlife is concerned, such as a pair of red-throated divers on Lochan an Ais below the road, but these days there is a tripod and telescope in the centre for visitors to get a closer view of the birds. A pair of pied wagtails were in the car park, a handsome male ring ouzel on the cliff, meadow pipits everywhere with many feeding young, and the croak of a raven overhead. My favourite place on the trail is a miniature cliff adjacent to the path and the moist conditions caused by the constant trickle of water over the rock face support large clumps of one of my favourite saxifrages: the yellow mountain saxifrage. The rock face is flanked by close-cropped grassland and heath where both the common and alpine lady's mantles grow in profusion and often side by side. The views, as always, were breathtaking with the hills of Cul Beag, Cul Mor and Stac Polly outlined against a blue sky and when I reached the northern end of the trail the tops of the two ridges of Suilven rose behind Cul Mor.

If it had not been for the fact that they were lying under a conifer I doubt whether I would have realised that what I was looking at were pine cones. Unopened cones of Arolla pine are easy to identify as cones although being round they are an unusual shape. When the cones have been opened up by a small mammal or bird, however, they look very strange with the whitish tiny hollows scattered all over the round object. Unlike other cones those of the Arolla pine do not open on their own accord but fall to the ground where they rot or await the attention of small mammals or birds who are after the seeds. As the seeds of this pine do not rely on the wind for assistance in spreading the seeds have no wings like other cones. This pine was introduced to Britain in 1746 by the Duke of Argyll. This was all fairly straightforward in reference books unlike the next tree which was a real puzzle.

It was a very large and tall beech tree but the upper three-quarters had thinly dissected leaves whilst the lower part had normal beech leaves. I could find nothing in my modest library about such a beech tree so rang the one person who could tell me – my son Ian who is in the Forestry Commission (as I will continue to call it) in the Research Section. He confirmed it was a beech and is known as the fern-leaved beech – an entirely new tree for me. This unusual beech is a continental form introduced in 1826 to a nursery in Surrey. Where branches are cut or damaged ordinary leaves can appear along with the intermediate forms because the plant is a 'chimaera' with inner tissues of ordinary beech overlaid by tissues of the fern-leaved form. Driving back from these exciting two trees I suddenly realised the heather moorland had started to flower. Crossed-leaved heath and bell heather have been out for some time but the flowering of ling means that unfortunately another summer is about to go and there have already been other signs such as the swifts that have gone.

Seeds of teasel were placed in pots last year and this year the plants were moved into a raised bed; they have been introduced into the garden in the hope of attracting goldfinches. The plants started to flower at the beginning of August and I had forgotten just how tiny are the pink flowers and the fact that they flower in a ring round the widest circumference of the flower head. The raised bed is right next to the bird table simply because that is the part of the garden that we see most from the house. One of the fascinating aspects of teasels is the small quantities of water that gather in the cups formed by the base of the leaves. Some insects become trapped in the liquid and once they have been broken down by bacteria it is possible the plant gains from the nutrients released. Birds will sometimes drink from this water, a fact recorded a long time ago by John Clare who in 1809 in a poem entitled *Noon* wrote

> By the hot relentless sun
> E'en the dew is parched up
> From the Teasel's jointed cup
> Oh poor birds, where must ye fly
> Now your water pots are dry.

The activity of birds on the bird table scattered seed around and some had fallen into the nearest teasel cups when an adult and juvenile great spotted woodpecker came to the nuts. The juvenile then flew on to the fence and then to our surprise flitted on to the stem of a teasel where it clung, taking seeds out of the cup. As for the goldfinches there are small numbers in the strath and very occasionally we have seen them on thistles in the garden but as for the teasels attracting them there may be a problem. Distribution maps show that in the wild teasels do not go any further north in Scotland than Perth which is over 100 miles (160 km) south of our garden. This means that the local goldfinches may not know what to do with this new addition of a seed source. Meanwhile it is unlikely that any birds will use the water in the cups as there is water under the bird table for them to drink and wash in whilst in the paddock there are the two ponds.

The idea of 'local behaviour' in birds may be more widespread than we think as I remember it happening when I was a Warden at Inverpolly National Nature Reserve on the Ross-shire – Sutherland border in 1969. The first thing I did in the garden was to hang out some peanuts on thick cotton with the nuts still in their shells. Weeks went by and not a single great or blue tit arrived and touched them. Then one morning I believe a new great tit arrived and immediately started attacking the shells and within a week every tit in the garden was doing the same. Perhaps as goldfinches are classed as 'partial migrants' in the Highlands, one day a pair might come along who know what to do with teasels so we will persist in growing them.

Achvaneran is also not far off the northern and western range as far as breeding goldfinches are concerned, and they are classified as local or sporadic in Valerie Thom's classic book *Birds in Scotland*. There is some flocking after the breeding season is over, and these are larger after dry summers have produced a good seed crop such as in the early 1970s, when flocks of up to 40 were seen on the Black Isle just north of Inverness. In contrast, after hard winters there is a general decrease in numbers. In this strath I have seen more than 15 birds together with all such records coming from the autumn or late summer when there is plenty of seed around. At other times of the year they are mainly in twos or threes, and once one fed at the bird table in the middle of winter.

Even a short drive over this island in the Western Isles and a short walk over the shell sand dunes known as the machair were enough to make you realise why so many people dread the spread of the mink from the islands of Lewis and Harris to the north. Some of the small crofting fields on the west coast of the island are dominated by buttercups, others by silverweed whilst others are rich assemblages of plants including ragged robin, marsh orchids, lady's smock, yellow rattle and eyebright. With the sun shining over these flower-rich fields the common blue, small heath and meadow brown butterflies were dancing over the blossoms. There are still areas of irises which afford protection to the corncrakes early in the season and now the crofters are being given financial incentives to alter their agricultural practices of recent years to give this rare bird a better chance. Corncrakes are so secretive that I knew there was virtually no chance of seeing one and I was right – I did not!

The cause for all the concern at the possibility of mink turning up is readily apparent as the internationally important numbers of ground-nesting waders would be at risk as well as the rare corncrake. Waders were simply everywhere with some flocks of lapwings already forming. At one point a buzzard flapped low over the fields and the adjoining machair and a series of birds rose up to mob it including redshank, oyster catcher, dunlin and lapwing. On the way back to the airport I stopped to look at a roadside loch on Benbecula as there were what I thought to be several pairs of mallard with their young. Through binoculars I watched tufted duck with ducklings, a little grebe and a single female gadwall that had perhaps lost her eggs or ducklings. I then looked at the so-called mallard and realised that they were all in fact shoveler. All these would be at risk if mink invaded these islands of the Uists and Benbecula and the proud cockerels with their hens next to the croft house would also go.

The hill lochan was over 100 acres (40 ha) in size which indicates that the only definition I have been able to find for the word lochan – a small area of water – is not very satisfactory; the translation of its Gaelic name is 'lochan of the red grouse'. There were plenty of signs of red grouse on the surrounding moorland but ironically the only grouse I saw were two male black grouse sitting in a birch tree over-hanging a small cliff face. The loch disturbed me because it was eerie and I felt uncomfortable as I stood at the bank fishing for brown trout. Perhaps it was the fact that despite the flat calm water I did not see a single 'dimple' of a trout rising, or perhaps it was the silence which even for the Highlands was impressive but for some reason disturbing. Despite its size there was not a single bird on the water, whereas at this time of the year there should have been at least mallard and tufted duck or even a Slavonian grebe as it was in the heart of this rare bird's breeding distribution.

For an hour I saw no sign of a fish and no sign of any water birds and then suddenly a rise to my left and at the second cast the fish was hooked. It took some time to get the fish in sight and I was amazed to see that it was in fact a pike, the first pike I have ever caught in the Highlands. It weighed just over 5 lbs (2 kg) and I was intrigued to see what it had been eating and it did not come as a sur-prise to find a duckling – unidentifiable – in its stomach. The presence of the pike in the lochan could well explain the lack of water birds and the lack of trout rising. Pike are not native to the Highlands and have over the years been introduced by coarse anglers who have seemed indifferent to the impact on native fish communities.

A combination of parsley, dill, cider, anchovies, garlic, butter and breadcrumbs brought out the surprisingly delicious flavour of the fried pike, well accompanied by a glass of claret.

At the Highland Field Sports Fair at Moy Hall near Inverness it was hard to tell who enjoyed the terrier racing the most – the onlookers or the dogs. The dogs seemed to be in their element and the races drew the largest crowd of the day to the main ring despite other attractions there such as falconry and gun dog displays. The terriers were put in release boxes and then the dummy started up and the boxes opened. In the first heat one of the terriers caught the dummy halfway up the ring and the resulting mêlée was chaotic with dogs everywhere; the heat had to be held again. A friend had a terrier in the next heat but as soon as the release box was opened his terrier darted round the back of the box and sat next to my friend's wife whilst it watched the other terriers racing. After the next heat it was obvious that a small brown terrier was the fastest although there was some strong opposition. The final started and the brown terrier was in front as the dummy sped up the ring. Unfortunately in the last few yards the brown terrier took an obvious dislike to a terrier to its left and attacked it and they were still squabbling when a much slower terrier crossed the line to win.

The two main topics of conversation amongst the crowds were the disastrous year for red grouse and some optimism over red deer. Whatever one thinks of red grouse shooting this year will see millions of pounds lost to the economy with so many estates cancelling their shooting days. In contrast there is some optimism with the over-population of red deer. Natural mortality in calves, the large number of hinds not even in calf and higher hind culls by some estates have halted the growth in population. Unfortunately too many people simply see the red deer problem in isolation when in reality what must also be taken into account are the roe deer and sika deer that are increasing in numbers and distribution and the ever ubiquitous sheep.

Nothing could have prepared me for the excitement of a wildlife incident in the latter part of July this year. I was sitting in a glade in woodland east of Inverness watching speckled wood butterflies fluttering erratically in and out of shade. In the glade was a small swarm of heath-spotted orchids, a single marsh orchid, a scattering of common wintergreen and two spikes of creeping lady's tresses. Earlier from the small woodland pond a pair of teal had splashed noisily from the water to be followed by a single mallard. A roe deer had moved away slowly through the trees as if it was not really disturbed by my presence. Moving on through the trees from the glade I had reached a very large birch when up from my feet rose a woodcock. I have flushed very many woodcock in the past and some of them – as this one – from about 2 ft (0.6 m) in front of me but this was a woodcock with a difference as it was carrying a young bird between its thighs. The young bird was pressed up against the bird's lower parts and I even saw the bill which was about 2 in (5 cm) long. This was the sight of a lifetime that people with much more experience of woodcock have never seen.

I then looked at my feet and there was a young bird that had been left behind. It was well grown and feathered and fluttered up as I looked closer so I moved quickly away. The adult bird had pitched down only about 30 yds (27 m) away but out of sight and I went in the opposite direction to stop any further disturbance. There has always been controversy as to whether woodcock really carry their young – in the books I have it has always been tiny chicks, not what in this case I would have called a young juvenile bird. Some people have claimed it has been accidental with a brooded chick being picked up as the adult rose to flight. In this case such a large young bird could not have been being brooded so it looks as though it was deliberate. I count myself a very lucky man!

On the Ordnance Survey map a few miles north of Alness and beside the A836 road is a field called a Drove Stance. When the cattle were moving through this part of the Highlands on their way to the trysts (fairs) further south they would have rested in the field, or stance as it was called. The cattle came down drove roads reaching up into the westerly and northerly Highlands from four main gathering points such as Reay and Ben More Assynt in Sutherland and Strath Halladale and Georgemas in Caithness. The cattle would scarcely resemble their modern counterparts, which are mainly large and red and sometimes hired out to hotels to graze for the visitors to see. The old droving cattle were much smaller and mainly black; few of these herds exist any more although I did see one on the island of Canna a few years ago. The next morning the cattle would move down to one of the main trysts of the north – established in about 1820 – at Beauly and later nearer Muir of Ord. Then they would push further south, ending up at even larger trysts like the ones at Crieff and Falkirk and for some cattle it did not even end there as they went down to Smithfield. Such droving existed for probably centuries but modern transport, refrigeration and the lack of demand as wars ended led to the demise of droving at the end of the nineteenth century.

I hoped that the reason the field had been spared from the surrounding conifer plantations was because of its historical significance. As I wandered across the field I wondered what it would have looked like when the cattle were resting there. They would not have been shod until further south when the harder roads were encountered. The field was damp with clumps of soft rush everywhere and in the wetter parts green and yellow sphagnum mosses dominated small areas. In other parts the swarms of heath-spotted orchids had gone over but there were still a few pearl-bordered fritillaries fluttering low over the vegetation.

There seemed to be dragonflies everywhere both over the water and over the heathers and sphagnum mosses between the water's edge and the birch woodland. Red damselflies and blue damselflies were paired off whilst others sluggishly clung to sedge stems where they had recently emerged from their nymph cases. Suddenly a much larger dragonfly flew past with a 3 in (8 cm) body and 4 in (10 cm) wing span and there a few feet in front of me was a golden ringed dragonfly. This is one of the only two dragonflies in the Highlands that lay their eggs in flowing water – the other is the much rarer beautiful demoiselle – and their nymphs dig themselves into the bed of a burn or river and wait for food to pass by. As the name suggests there are bands of gold and black on the abdomen. The rarest dragonfly on the loch that day was the brilliant emerald and several of them were hunting over the edge of the loch and flying quite fast.

Despite the beauty of the loch with all the aquatic plants and the dragonflies the 'stars' of the day had appeared when we first left the car and were walking down the lane. To start with I thought the animal at the roadside about 20 yds (18 m) away was a dog and then suddenly I realised it was in fact a roe deer kid. It was grazing on the roadside verge just outwith the birch trees and in plain view, as indeed we were, but it still carried on grazing. There was a constant flickering of the kid's ears because of the unwelcome attention of insects and the kid was gradually walking closer to us. At one point it stopped and looked directly at us but then carried on grazing. Suddenly there was a movement to the right of the kid and I thought it was the doe but, incredibly, it was another kid – twins grazing less than 20 yds (18 m) away and in the open. I was just spellbound and as the purpose of our visit was to record a tape for BBC Scotland, we just switched the microphone on and I described what was happening.

Dirrie Moor

The reason for visiting this large tract of open moorland a few miles south of Ullapool was to search for the dwarf birch (*Betula nana*). On the edge of the first loch a greenshank was calling with those notes that tells her chicks to stay and hide. The second wader of the day was a common snipe and it gives some idea of the dramatic fall in numbers in the Highlands that this was only the second snipe I have seen in the last two years. Eventually I found the dwarf birch – a group of around 30 and some of them had tiny catkins about half an inch long. I had last seen this tiny tree – the tallest specimen there was about 18 in (46 cm) high with most of them much smaller – on my last expedition to Iceland. I had forgotten just how small the leaves were as they were smaller than the size of a five pence piece with distinctly scalloped margins. Parts of the moorland were splashed with colour from such plants as heath-spotted orchid, the white and pink forms of lousewort, the delicate shade of thyme whose leaves I crushed and smelt and the yellow of lady's bedstraw.

I pushed across undulating moorland, fording two wide burns on the way and then climbed up the extensive push moraine. From there looking north-west a large loch lay at the foot of Beinn Dearg which rose to over 3000 ft (914 m). I had been told that the dwarf birch was widespread in the area but although I walked for about 2 miles (3 km) the original 'grove' of tiny trees were the only ones I could locate. Going back a different route I found the nest of a red grouse with eggs scattered around with a single hole where the hooded crow would have predated them. Back on the road I found three casualties at the roadside: the first was a juvenile meadow pipit and the other two were surprises as they were both red admiral butterflies. I must go back to the dwarf birch in the autumn as their leaves can be as bright as the colours on the much larger silver birch.

The two African pygmy goats have not liked the hot weather and have shown this in a number of ways which reflect their different characters and temperaments. The silver blue goat called Treasure is both more dominant and belligerent and if there is any stamping or snorting going on it will more often than not be her. She will often drive away the brown and white goat, Trivia, from the last piece of food especially if it is a titbit such as willow herb which both of them love. In early summer we had two evenings when the midges were bad and I went to the expense of buying some repellent that I had been told would work and keep the midges away from the goats. The idea was to spread the liquid thinly over my hands and then run them over the backs and side of the goats. Strangely enough the bottle was never opened as we have since had no midges to speak of despite horrific stories about them from the west coast this year. In the heat both goats would sit facing each other under the shade of the fruit trees but if it is really hot they both retire into their shed which surprisingly enough is cool.

Neither of the goats has grown very much since they have been with me as Treasure is only 21 in (53 cm) at the shoulder and Trivia is even smaller at 20 in (51 cm). The two nannies have their goat mix three times a day and I love to sit on a rock in the middle of their enclosure and have their muzzles deep in my hands after the food. Two friends came two weeks ago to worm both goats and look at their feet; I have difficulty in handling them as I am frightened of hurting them. Fortunately the huge rock in their enclosure which they run up and down as if in a game has meant that their feet were worn away naturally so there was no need to use the savage-looking cutters. More people stop and peer over the fence at the goats than ever before and the children are always so curious and fascinated at such small goats – pygmies indeed.

Mushrooms are so uncommon in the Highlands now that I cannot mention exactly where 'my' mushroom field lies as others would be out after them. This year I was surprised to find the first crop just before the heatwave ended and I gathered enough for two helpings although I had to search for them. Then there were three days of virtually non-stop rain and on the third day a quick look revealed large numbers of mushrooms and I was out gathering them in the rain before anyone else saw them! I am a coward as far as eating fungi is concerned as apart from the field mushroom I have only ventured into chanterelles and occasionally shaggy ink caps although I have had unfortunate experiences with both. Many years ago a friend of mine in Lincolnshire used to invite me round for a proper jugged hare on the dinner menu. It was at one of these that I tried my first shaggy ink caps and I was very ill afterwards with hallucinations which might have resulted from the combination of the fungi and wine. Exactly the same thing happened to me once with chanterelles and I have tried to avoid both ever since.

But of the mushrooms I gathered last week I had some for breakfast and I had forgotten just how delicious they are compared with those from the supermarket which by comparison seem tasteless. I had also forgotten the fragrance of mushrooms and I could smell them even as I was taking black and white photographs of them in the kitchen. Mushrooms have, since ancient times, been regarded as food for the gods and the Egyptian pharaohs thought they passed on magical powers. Many people thought they held health-giving properties but my own feelings about them are that they are as magical as the brown hares which run over the fields where I collected them. Mushrooms were the favourite food of the Emperor Claudius who conquered southern Britain in the first century. He even had a mushroom, *Amanita caesarea*, named after him.

It looked incongruous striding along a sun-soaked beach near Inverness where people were sunbathing as I had wellingtons on and was carrying a long-handled pond net. Not so my two grandchildren as they were in their element running through the shallow water as we headed for the rocks. There are few rock pools on this part of the east coast of the Highlands but this stretch is ideal as some of them are deep. The main purpose of the visit was to collect some winkles for me to eat and the pond net was to introduce the children to the rich wildlife of the pools. When I was their age I was brought up on elvers (baby eels), tripe and chitterlings with the occasional bag of winkles that were sold from a market stall in Gloucester. A few years ago when I kept several aquariums my favourite was the one for rock pool fish, anemones and crabs and it was at Rosemarkie that I collected the various specimens.

Once a good bag of winkles had been collected I started pond dipping, trying to remember the technique I had used in the past when looking for sticklebacks and newts. For a while I caught nothing but the inevitable winkles, but then the first small crab appeared and went into the glass jar for a while. Then the first fish and one of my favourites in the aquarium as it was a 15-spined stickleback. The specimens I had caught before were about 6 in (15 cm) long and resembling a miniature pike but this one was very young as it was only about an inch long. A larger crab came next and then two blennies from a deep pool near the crashing waves and then a goby to complete the catch for the morning. The catch was carefully released into a large pool where there were dozens of red anemones, many with their tentacles out and looking almost bizarre. The following day I had the winkles for lunch with garlic butter; they were delicious; they reminded me of the days when elvers were so cheap to buy that some people gave them away!

Red squirrels have few predators in the Highlands although occasionally no doubt a fox or a wildcat catches one off its guard. Several people have claimed that pine martens have wiped them out in some areas but there is no evidence to support this and it is more likely to be fragmentation of woodland by housing or clearance. Road casualties are a problem but recently there was a much more unusual casualty on the south side of Loch Ness. On both wooded shores of the loch red squirrels are still fairly common and the nearest grey squirrels are, fortunately, still a long way away. Last week a dead red squirrel was found under a large tree whose branches were very close to electricity wires. The red squirrel still had some moss in its mouth so would have died instantly from the electric shock and burn marks were clearly seen. The Hydro Board have been approached to solve the problem.

The plight of the red squirrel in Britain has been highlighted recently by a consortium of conservation bodies and with this in mind it is interesting to reflect on the history of this species in the Highlands. Severe winters and loss of habitat resulted in the probable extinction of red squirrels in the Highlands in the eighteenth century. If this was the case then all the red squirrels in the Highlands at present are descendants from introductions of English stock in the nineteenth century. However by the turn of the present century the red squirrels were so abundant they were causing enormous damage to woodland. So the Highland Squirrel Club was formed in 1903 covering parts of Ross-shire, Sutherland and Inverness-shire. During the following 15 years 60,450 red squirrels were killed. The record was in 1909 when 7199 red squirrels were taken. The bounty on the tails was three or four pence each. If they became extinct again in the Highlands we could, perhaps, not turn to England for them as it seems likely they would be extinct there too.

Tibbles – as she came to be called – was probably dumped in the strath and we saw the cat for the first time in the autumn of last year. At first she would not come for food although she regularly visited the garden where she ignored all the poultry and, as far as we could see, the wild birds. How she managed to survive last winter is a mystery as in January temperatures dropped to −26°C. Then a few months ago she started to visit the garden more and more nonchalantly, ignoring the five dachshunds when they went walkabouts. A few weeks ago she started coming for food when her name was called but she would not come too close.

Tibbles always left the garden in the same direction and then we saw her three kittens in woodland half a mile away. The tiny kittens were so young they were unlikely to survive as, despite being mid September, some nights the temperature had already dropped to −5°C. There was also the fact that the cat would simply carry on having more kittens.

Following consultation with the SSPCA and Cat Rescue we decided to trap Tibbles and a piece of quail meat enticed her into a humane trap and she was then placed in my study. It took half an hour to find the kittens because although the first one was asleep in long grass the other two were 4 ft (1.2 m) down a rabbit hole; then they were reunited with their mother. The first thing Tibbles did was to clean up the kittens and to our amazement all three were pure white. To our surprise she then introduced them to the dirt box and they have used it ever since.

Homes will have to be found for all three kittens, Tibbles will be taken to the vet for an operation and then if she wants to come in so be it as she can join our other four cats. As I write this Tibbles is trying to get some sleep but with three kittens bouncing around the room she has little chance.

Common Frog

Autumn

The rock pools appeared to be small worlds of their own between the tide and the seaweeds in them varied colours that included green, brown, red and yellow. Between the fronds were the bright red beadlet anemones whose loose tentacles were often open whilst in contrast small crabs were well hidden until disturbed. It was an idyllic scene with oystercatchers still piping away although their breeding season was long over. In the firth the calm conditions were unusual and it was easy to see the distant long-tailed ducks and red-breasted mergansers. Then suddenly the calm surface was broken as dolphins rose gracefully and sometimes in unison, their grey bodies arched above the water.

But it was back to the rock pools for us as we were collecting for our marine aquarium using a net. Most books an marine aquariums go into detail as to how difficult it is to maintain aquariums so we compromised by having a rock pool aquarium. Marine life in rock pools is far more flexible over water conditions as between tides rain often reduces the salinity levels considerably before the tide invades yet again.

A few small crabs went into the collecting bucket along with several shells to feed the starfish we already have in the aquarium in our dining room. But by then we were a little frustrated, as having set up a basic aquarium we were after some fish. Then in the lower rock pools just above the gently lapping waves we caught a 15-spined stickleback nearly 6 in (15 cm) long. These are magnificent fish that look like minature pike but with scales of silver and brown rather like armour plating. Then came a scorpion fish followed by a bearded rockling and then another stickleback so the catch was sufficient and it was home as soon as possible.

As the helicopter passed over the north west tip of mainland Scotland I asked the pilot if I could take some aerial photographs when we reached North Rona, some 46 miles (74 km) further to the north east. Nothing could have prepared me for the moment when I knelt down with camera ready and the large door slid open and there I was staring down on to the island. It was so awe-inspiring and, I admit, frightening that I nearly forgot what I was supposed to be doing. On landing I made for the huge grey seal rookery scattered across a north-reaching peninsula and was soon photographing combinations of bulls, cows and pups. There were plenty of white pups scattered throughout the colony and some were a long way from the sea and well up the lower slopes of the hill. As with St Kilda it is believed that the rookery did not form until the people were evacuated – in the case of North Rona in 1844 – and now the rookery produces 2000 pups each year.

Standing on this isolated, storm-lashed island it was difficult to imagine that the 300 acres (120 ha) once supported as many as 30 people. The only signs that remain are a sheep fank, a few crumbling earth houses and an area of lazy beds. An even earlier occupation has left the ruins of St Ronan's cell from the ninth century AD and a medieval chapel. Both the latter structures were partly restored by Fraser Darling during his famous four months' stay on the island in 1938. As it was November there were no auks around but I was surprised at the numbers of fulmars – as if they did not realise the breeding season was over. Other birds included the great black-backed gulls scavenging amidst the seal rookery whilst elsewhere small groups of redwings – the dark Icelandic race – sought shelter as did a single golden plover and snow bunting. Then it was time to go and I realised that even at this time of the year North Rona was as stimulating and exciting as my last visit in June.

Even as I stood on the airstrip near Kyle on the mainland opposite Skye the weather in the west was worsening and I guessed it would be my third abortive trip to St Kilda this year. The wind was strong enough to keep a female merlin quite low, just skimming the grassland next to the hangar and then in came the helicopter with a deafening rush of air. The pilot confirmed my fears but did say that we could get out for a meeting on Benbecula and if the weather held we could have an aerial view of the seals on the Monach Isles. I had been keen on this if only to assess erosion damage to the sand dune system as there is a large breeding rookery of grey seals each year.

Then we were off and over the sea in minutes and into squally showers that buffeted the small helicopter as if to illustrate the power of the elements. The flight was a series of dramatic images to the eye: the huge trawler with a cloud of gulls enveloping it; grey stone shells of houses where entire crofting communities had long since gone; a waterfall tumbling over a sea cliff only to have the water pushed upwards by the force of the wind. Our route took us over a part of the Western Isles that seems to be more water than land and the almost total absence of trees was noticeable. The numerous lochs and lochans support a few birds in the winter but most are desolate apart from the occasional wildfowl. We disturbed a small party of greylag geese that flew south but these were the only birds I saw before we touched down at Benbecula.

With the meeting over it was out over the Monach Isles that lay like green lawns against a background of the wind lashed seascape. Then there were suddenly seals everywhere – hauled out on stony outcrops or resting in small pools but with the majority on the beach. There were hundreds of mixed cows, pups and bulls, but as far as I could see they were not on the small areas of erosion so it was more likely to have been caused by the elements – wind and sea.

On the second day in October the hills of Glen Affric were topped with mist on a windless day with no ripple on even the largest loch. We walked for miles looking at the lochs and lochans of this famous Forestry Commission area so that we could advise them on management for dragonflies. With 14 species of dragonflies at one lochan it is one of the richest areas in the north of Scotland so it is fortunate that the Commission's remit for wildlife conservation has changed in recent years. Despite the distance and beautiful scenery there was little sign of wildlife apart from the red deer, a single red grouse and the distant ominous croak of a raven. Most of the area we walked was over rough, leggy heather but remnants of old Caledonian pine forest clothed some of the landscape and the old 'granny' pines were spectacular and contrasted with the changing colours of the rowan trees.

Curlew

Then suddenly we came to an area no different from the miles behind us but wildlife seemed everywhere. A mixed party of birds moving through a small, regenerated pine area included coal, great and blue tits with at least two crested tits and a single tree creeper. A late wheatear – perhaps the Greenland race – flitted along a track in front and then a family party of long-tailed tits broke cover and chattered all around us. In a small lochan was a frog whilst on the margins were hundreds of tiny toadlets from what must have been a very late spawn. A dead female common hawker dragonfly lay at the water's edge but overhead three males were circling and feeding on tiny insects. Then two started a fight and such was their aggression that they fell to the ground and we could hear the thrashing of wings some distance away. I was able to pick up one of the combatants and point out identification features to my companions and then on its release the hawker flew up to the trees where it was promptly attacked by a willow warbler. However at the last minute the warbler changed its mind as if it had suddenly realised just how large a prey it had chosen.

We saw few deer because they were all downwind of us but their impressions in the grass and heather indicated where they had lain. Then a red deer stag roaring in a distant corrie indicated that the rut was under way although it was still early days.

Two months ago a local naturalist brought me a small mammal to identify as he could not work out which species he had obtained. The animal had been brought in by a cat that had been hunting along the shoreline of Loch Ness. The blunt nose indicated it was a vole but the specimen was too large to have been a bank vole or field vole and in any case the tail was too long. However the tail was far too short to have been a brown rat and the ears and muzzle were also too short. So by a process of elimination it could only have been a water vole. However this was no ordinary water vole as it was completely black rather than the more usual brown colour. This black form – some people claim it to be a distinct subspecies, *Arvicola terrestris reta* – is only occasionally found in Britain and generally in the north of Scotland. To be fair to the naturalist who brought the specimen to me it is unusual to see a black form and the size aspect was not readily apparent as it was immature.

The distribution maps for the water vole indicate that the location where this particular vole was found is at the extreme northern edge of its known range, although it is suspected to occur even further north and west. Although I have not seen a live water vole in the Highlands, I have occasionally found them as prey items in golden eagle eyries and these have always been the black form. This is another indication of the wide range of food that golden eagles will take. Other predators on the water voles include stoat, mink and pike. Water voles are therefore uncommon throughout the Highlands and do not seem to occur at all in the Inner or Outer Hebrides. So most people I spoke to had never seen a water vole, let alone a black one and there was considerable interest in the specimen – so much interest, in fact, that I decided to have the specimen mounted. The end result is a very attractive and interesting mount with the animal on a small log, upright in the feeding position.

Television can bring far off places into our homes and we tend to get used to some of the exotic species from abroad; in this connection I was watching the small screen where flightless cormorants from the Galapagos Islands were the subject of attention. I wonder how many people realise that in the early part of the nineteenth century Britain had its own flightless bird before it was hunted to extinction. This sea bird, the great auk, was also called the garefowl and was much bigger by far than any of our existing auks. It was its size that impressed me when I first saw a mounted skin in the Reykjavik Museum in Iceland. It struck me as resembling an overgrown razorbill but it was not far short of 3 ft (1 m) high with very small wings. It was not until quite recently that the species impressed me yet again because in the Inverness Museum I was shown two of the magnificent eggs of the great auk. They were 5 in (13 cm) in length and 3 in (8 cm) in diameter but covered with brown blotches and looking like an overgrown guillemot or razorbill egg. There has even been a book written describing all the known great auk eggs in the world.

Its former range was once over the North Atlantic from America to Europe and it bred on islands round the coast of Scotland. However its range in Scotland is not known although remains found in kitchen middens in Caithness, Oronsay and the Orkneys indicate it could have been widespread round the coasts. Known breeding sites include Papa Westray where a female with an egg was stoned to death around 1812 and the male was killed in 1813 with the skin being deposited in the British Museum. As far as we know the last British record is of one caught on Stac an Armin, St Kilda, where it was killed as a witch. The last record was in June 1844 when a pair was killed at Elday, Iceland – the pair had an egg. The persecution was originally for food but towards the end, as with a few other species, it was the eggs and skins that were taken to sell to avid collectors.

This archipelago lies 8 miles (13 km) west of North Uist in the Western Isles and they cover an area of about 600 acres (240 ha). They are known locally as Heisker but the Monach name was adopted by the Admiralty to avoid confusion with the nearby island of Haskeir. At one time – as is the case with many of these smaller islands – they were occupied with, in 1891, 135 people including 24 lighthousemen and fishermen. But by 1943 the people had gone and these low – maximum height is 50 ft (15 m) – islands were left to the grey seals. For the seals the sandy beaches mixed with rocky shorelines were ideal for having pups and mating and once the disturbance and killing by the islanders had stopped they were quick to exploit the situation. Thousands of grey seals gather at this rookery each October and it was to see this scene that I visited the islands in mid October this year.

As I lay on sand dunes and peered through marram grass the bulls, cows and pups below me was one of the most spectacular wildlife sights I have seen for a long time. But my visit was not to admire the seals but to check if any showed signs of being affected by virus and it was a relief to find no sign of this, although we took blood samples to check for its presence. There were a few dead pups but this was only to be expected with the numbers involved. Another purpose was to see if the seals were causing any erosion in the sand dunes and this again appeared negative although aerial photography will prove or disprove this. What seemed to be happening was that the grey seal cows were using the natural erosion to give shelter to their still-white pups, as some of these were a long way from the sea. Then I had time to stalk a small rookery in a sheltered bay, stalking with a camera and seeing a cow deftly wrap its flipper round a pup and draw it in to feed on milk. In contrast two large bulls fought at the water's edge with blood flowing.

This is the name of our house and it is marked as such on Ordnance Survey 1:50,000 maps. When we moved here just over a year ago we were determined to find out something about the history of the building. Fortunately just as we started making enquiries the reprint of the first edition of the Ordnance Survey was extended from England to cover Scotland and we were intrigued to find the name Achvaneran on the map. This set the first puzzle, however, as the map was surveyed between 1866 and 1872 with a revision in 1894. So the house was at least there in 1894 and possibly long before. Whilst we deliberated on this fact one other piece of information came our way in that we found out that the word Achvaneran is Gaelic for Field of the Milkmaids. This conjured up various images in our minds as it linked in with the two large stones in the garden with a metal ring in the top. These two stones would have been part of a cheese press and used to press out the moisture and we presumed it was of the freestanding type rather than built into the outer wall of the house as there was no sign where it could have been.

Then more information came to light about when the house was built and – as is often the case – by a chance meeting. I attended a demonstration of vehicle winches on a marshy area near Inverness and after the event I was talking to the farmer who owned the land. When I told him where we lived he told me that his mother had lived at Achvaneran until 1900 when she moved up the hill for a few months whilst the house – which was thatched – was pulled down and the existing house built in its place. All this is fascinating but it makes us even more determined to find out yet more such as when the huge beech and sycamores were planted and what were the banks and stones under the trees. Then there is the old stone building – a bothie as it would have been called – halfway down the slope, perhaps used for stock although it has a stone floor.

The use of plants as badges by most Scottish clans goes back to at least 1600 and possibly much earlier although the formalisation of their use did not happen until about 1822 when they were registered at Lyon Court in Edinburgh. This is where the Lyon Register is maintained – the Public Register of All Arms and Bearings in Scotland. A sprig was worn either on its own, behind the crest on a bonnet or on a staff. The choice of plants seems to have depended on a number of factors from a mere whim to the role of such a plant in folklore or even because it was abundant in the countryside or had a practical use. Some of the plants have a reputation for protection from evil such as the juniper of the Murrays or holly – a very powerful plant against evil in all its forms – that was used by both the Drummonds and Macmillans. Heather was chosen by the MacAlisters and Macdonalds although the Macphersons stipulated white heather. Heather is an obvious choice because it was so abundant and from a practical point of view was so important with a variety of uses from making rope to thatch and besoms to orange dye. Heather beds were so springy that many of the Highland settlers in North America took their heather beds with them, so introducing heather to the New World.

The choice of the plant did not always follow the beliefs of the time and such was the case with the aspen of the Fergussons. The tree was generally shunned by the Scots and considered a cursed tree because its leaves tremble in even the slightest breeze. Legend has it that the tree could never rest as its wood was used for the cross and it was the only tree that held up its head, whilst others bowed, during the procession to Calvary. The leaves tremble so much because their thin leaf stalks are so long but whatever the reason in the old days crofters and fishermen would not use the wood for their gear. Perhaps if the timber had been more usable in carpentry terms the whole story could have been different.

Such plant badges are unusual these days but when the Duke of Atholl's ceremonial bodyguard – the only 'private army' in the country – assemble on formal occasions each man wears a sprig of juniper because, after all, there may be lots of devils, elves and witches around and there is nothing like juniper for protection against such beings.

The other tree that affords even more protection against evil is the rowan. They were often planted in gardens to ward of evil spirits and this may be the reason why it was the plant badge of the Malcolms and Menzies, although the former specified rowan berries whilst the latter had a small sprig. In Scottish folklore only the birch – renowned as a symbol of fertility – is more important than the rowan. However there is a certain magic about the rowan and so much so that, unlike birch, people will not cut rowans down as it is supposed to bring bad luck. Some people will not even trim branches however inconvenient they may be. I personally would not go that far but certainly could not bring myself to actually cut one down.

The plant badge of the Ramsays was the harebell or bluebell, but this is not a choice of one or the other as it only refers to *Campanula rotundifolia*, whose correct Scottish name is bluebell although elsewhere it is known as the harebell. The plant badge of the MacLennans must have been a prickly one as it is gorse, more often called whins in the Highlands, although some people refer to it as a furze. If these plant badges went behind the crest on a bonnet or on a staff the MacKays must have had a problem with the bulrush especially when it started shedding its fine seeds!

The Gairloch Conservation Unit was one of the first 'deer units' to be formed – in 1967 – and its initial objective was the 'integrated management of red deer over the area covered by the five estates'. The area is approximately 100,000 acres (40,000 ha) set in some of the wildest landscape of Wester Ross and is bounded to the north-east by Loch Maree, to the north, west and south by the sea and Loch Torridon and then by deer fencing from Loch Maree to Glen Torridon. As the present secretary of the GCU I went to the last meeting held in the Anancaun Field Station on the edge of Beinn Eighe National Nature Reserve and as always I was impressed by the members of the unit.

Landowners, Forestry Commission, National Trust for Scotland and Nature Conservancy Council representatives sat around the table and as usual I found the conversation more than stimulating. It was not only deer that were being discussed, as the range of subjects included Soay sheep, foxes, golden eagle, stoat and buzzard and it felt good to be in the company of people who knew so much about the wildlife of the surrounding landscape and beyond. But deer were the main subject of the formal session including a discussion on the latest deer fencing in the unit, the increasing numbers of sika deer being culled and the heavy natural mortality of red deer on the estates earlier in the year.

Photographs were passed round of the spring mortality that had been caused by long periods of wet weather lowering the resistance of deer to parasites. The photographs showed small groups of deer that had lain down and died, sometimes touching each other as they perhaps huddled together for warmth. Even the most hardened person in the room was moved by what they saw. Fortunately the unit does not have an over-population like many other areas in the Highlands and this is because each year the cull figures for red deer stags and hinds are worked out. The landowners are expected to keep to those figures and the years of being strict about this have paid off and the unit does not have the problems of most of the Highlands. Driving back through the vagaries of Highland weather I was still keyed up and stimulated until I suddenly remembered I had not taken enough notes to write out the minutes and that put everything into perspective!

Goat Moth

The two ponds in the garden dried up early in the summer and with a limited water supply from a spring up the hill beyond the birch trees there was no way we could fill the ponds from the household tap, particularly as three other houses rely on the same spring. The Indian runner ducks, khaki campbells and geese were not amused and their tracks criss-crossed the mud that formed for a while after any rain. We kept two large bowls full of water down near all the hutches but it was but little consolation to the birds, especially the geese as they were just too big to get into the bowls. It was ironic that a burn flowed constantly just outside two boundary fences of the paddock but I could not think of a way to utilise this source of water. Then my wife suggested a plastic pipe – which I did not think would work – but a 50 yd (46 m) length took the water, with the farmer's permission, from the burn into the ponds; for the rest of the summer it has trickled in and kept both ponds brimming over.

The ducks and geese were delighted but it has produced a constant battle between the ducks and me which they are slowly but surely winning. They constantly peck away at the margins of the pond where the water overflows and when a breach is made the water level drops and I have to repair the damage. However the consolation of seeing seven large Embden/Toulouse geese, 11 Indian runners and four khaki campbells on the water at one time is more than enough even though the battle over the defences may be lost. With the coming of the shorter days the egg production has dropped and even the brown laying hens have slowed down. Eight hen's eggs, six duck eggs and six quail eggs is a good day now but the worrying time of the year has begun as the predators can take advantage of the longer nights. Both stoat and pine marten have been in the garden recently and the pine marten – to the annoyance of the dachshunds – left its calling card on the kitchen doorstep.

At first sight the loch and its surrounding moorland looked desolate and even more so because large areas of ice were interspersed with areas of mirrow-calm open water. The island – with its ruins of Castle Lochindorb – was ringed with white ice that had accumulated round its margins but it was out near the island that we saw our first bird. A drake goldeneye was swimming away from the island and its contrasting black and white plumage was clearly reflected in the water. Near the bank there was a small group of tufted duck spending more time under the water than on the surface. One female had so large an area of white feathers at the base of the bill that in other circumstances I would have thought it must be a female scaup but I have been fooled in this way before. In the centre of the loch and so far out they were only seen through binoculars were the gooseganders – six males in superb plumage – and on putting the telescope on them it was easy to see why they are one of my favourite ducks. Despite the distance I could see the bottle-green head feathers, the thin red bill, and the pinkish tinge on the white body feathers was as pink as I ever remember seeing it before.

Away from the loch we could hear red grouse calling from various directions and then two appeared at the side of the road which was being gritted. Then we started to search the surrounding moorland looking away at any white stones to try and turn them into mountain hares in their winter coats. But this time they were indeed all stones and the only mountain hares we saw were three dead ones on the roads. But then we had the sighting of the day, as well up on the boulder-strewn slope the tribe of feral goats came into view. We had seen them there before but not in such numbers, as a count indicated 46 with the very good chance of a few others being out of sight. There were nannies, billies and kids that had been born in January or February this year.

We had meant to take the inflatable boat out to the Monach Isles but even as we flew from Stornoway to Benbecula the way the wind was affecting the Twin Otter plane meant the chance of the trip was nil. The weather was appalling even for the Western Isles and what rock doves I did see were having great difficulty in their balancing act on the stooks that were still in some of the narrow fields. The first surprise of the day was to see what I could only think was a male crossbill which flew up from the roadside where it had no doubt been feeding on seeds. Normally this would be a very unusual record but the invasion of the Outer Isles by crossbills has been extraordinary this year with birds present for several weeks even on St Kilda. The waves on the lochs we passed were so big that those duck that had not sought the sanctuary of reed and sedge beds were more out of sight than visible as they bobbed up and down. A peninsula jutting out into the sea on the west side gave us a vantage point to see magnificent waves and spray in which only the gannets seemed at home as there was a steady passage of adults and immature birds southwards. Two gannets I watched actually flew through a great mass of spray but they both shook their heads and carried on purposefully.

The highlight of the day was to find seven grey phalaropes feeding on the edge of the sea in a sheltered bay. This highlight was not because of the birds' rarity – only the second ones I have seen in Britain – but because of their delightful behaviour. The birds were feeding in quite shallow water but deep enough for them to be swimming and it seemed as though they were picking up insects that were being disturbed by the incoming waves. Several times they carried out that fascinating behaviour of phalaropes, pirouetting in tight circles on the water to form a mini whirlpool that brought food up to the surface judging by the frantic pecking that ensued when this was carried out. One of the birds that we took to be an adult was much paler than the others which had some brown on the head and back and we thought these to be birds of the year, but whatever age or sex they were they made us forget the elements for several magical moments as they danced and swam amidst the foam and water seeking food.

We then moved to the Loch Druidibeg National Nature Reserve to discuss the latest problem over red deer which had been introduced onto adjoining ground some years ago. The problem was that the deer found the lush vegetation on the small islands of the main loch to their liking, and as the water was so shallow the deer simply walked out to any island they wanted – or swam as the case may be. It was suspected, though not proven, that the grazing of the vegetation meant that there was a shortage of long grass in which the greylag geese could build their nests and this was the reason that the number of greylags breeding on the reserve had decreased. I suspected that the reason for the decline was more likely to be that they had spread to other parts of the Uists but again there was no proof.

The matter of red deer had come to a head a few years earlier when the stalker of the Nature Conservancy Council went to look at the problem and prompty shot a few deer! He was well within his rights to do this, but it was not deemed to be good policy but it did make the factor try and control the movements of the deer by disturbing them when they tended to wander to the loch. I have known red deer swim across huge lochs on the mainland when they can get grazing, especially on wooded islands. They swim very low in the water with just the head and top of the neck out of the water and they can get quite exhausted. They generally swim when the water is very calm and once they are on the island, if they do not want to leave, they just stay there and will largely ignore any efforts at getting them to swim off.

Mid November is not a time I normally visit this archipelago but it has its own fascination despite the absence of so many of the one million sea birds that breed on the islands during the summer months. Walking up through the village on the main island of Hirta there were turnstones feeding just a few feet away and apparently unconcerned at my proximity to them. Fulmars – inevitably – swept past my head within a few feet as their effortless flight took them to and from the cliff ledges where they were in their thousands despite the time of year. In the last few years on Hirta they have taken over new breeding sites such as the old quarry, the gabions protecting the low cliff near the pier from erosion and also the numerous cleitean scattered throughout the village. At first light that morning I had seen a hen foraging for food in our garden as I was feeding the ducks so I had a mental image of its size and colour and so when I found a St Kilda wren singing from the side wall of a cleit I could easily appreciate its much larger size and darker colouring. This island subspecies had been so reduced in numbers by the end of the nineteenth century because of over-collecting of birds and eggs that it was given special protection in 1904 by an Act of Parliament.

The Soay sheep in the village seem to fit in with the old grey walls of the houses along Main Street and it was interesting to watch the behaviour of the groups of several females and one or two males. Although it was towards the end of the rut the males were still trying to entice the females by nudging the sides of their flanks and raising a foreleg. There is no harem-type system as in red deer, as the Soay sheep are promiscuous.

Other birds included a pair of greylag geese that flew down from the fields of the village on to the sea but the surprise of the day was two jackdaws which flew over the village as there has been only a handful of records of this species on St Kilda this century.

The estate lies about 40 miles (64 km) south of Inverness adjacent to the A9 and runs to the west where it marches with Coignafearn in Strathdearn. We had been driven by Land Rover up the roughest of tracks until we reached around 1000 ft (305 m) where we had superb views of open moorland stretching for miles around with the highest ridges having a dusting of snow that reflected the bright lighting. It was satisfying to see good muirburn as the landscape was a mosaic of long narrow burnt strips of varying ages. This gives young shoots for the red grouse to feed on but nearby, and equally important, longer heather as cover for the birds should a predator such as a golden eagle appear. As we climbed out of the vehicle two roe deer

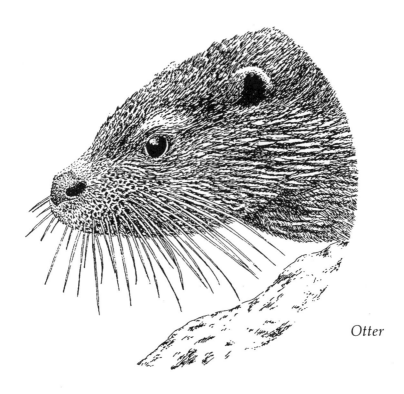

Otter

were grazing on a steep heather bank and indicating the changing habits of these small deer in that they were miles from the nearest tree cover. Then, as if to order, a peregrine falcon stooped in front of us at a red grouse but although the bird was struck it was not seriously hurt and managed to land and evade the falcon which flew on over the next snow-capped ridge.

The walk of about 3 miles (5 km) gave us an insight into the large number of red grouse and mountain hares and as regards the former I was intrigued at the grouse butts. Butts vary with the old-fashioned type that blend in with the landscape actually being marked on the 1:25000 Ordnance Survey maps. The type I looked at at Balavil were new butts and although they utilised some timber they were still sunk in the ground and used peat banks to blend into the moorland. At least they were far superior to the recent innovations in other areas of a few horizontal planks more like the American 'blinds'.

During the walk it was evident that the ground held a remarkable number of mountain hares with some of them in their brownish grey autumn coats whilst others were in white winter coats, contrasting against the dark moorland. There were no black hares and the estate had never heard of this unusual form that occurred in south-east Caithness. During our walk a pair of ravens were calling most of the time especially when a buzzard drifted through their winter territory. I still cannot find out why the collective name of ravens is an 'unkindness'.

The fox was on the hill and was worrying a small group of red deer hinds although they did not seem concerned apart from occasionally flicking their hooves at the animal. A stalker watched this performance for about 20 minutes and then the fox moved on to worry a sheep and after a while the stalker shot the fox. Such shooting is normally not an unusual event in the Highlands but there was something different about this particular fox and later that day the stalker rang me to see if I could go over and confirm identification as he thought it could be an arctic fox! As I drove to the deer larder several miles up a strath amidst the glorious colours of the autumn despite the threatening rain, I could not bring myself to believe that I might be about to look at an arctic fox that had been shot in the Highlands. I thought of a rare breed of dog or a red fox with mange but to my amazement there hanging in the larder was a real arctic fox.

It had a pure white bushy tail and a greyish body and was an immature male weighing only 12 lbs (5 kg) with plenty of fat. Arctic foxes have long been extinct in the Highlands after their initial colonisation after the last ice age so there was some discussion as to the origin of this particular specimen. Before my visit to the strath I had spoken to the Highland Wildlife Park at Kingussie where one of their arctic foxes had unfortunately been deliberately released some months back. That arctic fox had been found dead on a nearby main road so that source was ruled out. It was possibly somebody's pet that had not been recorded as missing or perhaps someone had taken one from a private collection somewhere down south and misguidedly released it in the Highlands; this had happened before although there had been a great deal of publicity at the time. More worrying, however, was the possibility that someone was ill-advisedly trying to recolonise the Highlands and more than one arctic fox had been released.

This freshwater loch lies a few miles east of Inverness and is one of the places we visit to count wildfowl during the winter and in the summer to see breeding coot and moorhen, both relatively uncommon in the Highlands. Occasionally, such as this year, a pair of Slavonian grebes will nest but to us a moorhen is just as attractive to watch despite the grebe's outstanding plumage. When we lived in England we may not have given a moorhen a second look although I have always likened its gait across grassland to what Toad of Toad Hall would have looked like as he strode across the countryside! Apart from the Slavonian grebe, which is not very rare locally, it is not often we see a rare species but the main purpose of our visits is to 'keep our eyes in' as regards identification. With a range of waterfowl it also gives an insight as to what is happening in the local scene as far as birds are concerned.

A road running close to the loch affords close views when using the car as a hide but we still take the telescope along to see the birds on the far edge of the loch. On our last visit many wigeon had come in from the nearby Beauly Firth and we counted 124 including many males in their splendid plumage with their subtle golden crowns. These ducks were scattered over the loch, mixing freely with the other species present although there were two concentrations of around 30 birds. In contrast the 24 mute swans were in a long double line as if spaced by an unknown hand apart from one unfortunate bird. We had seen this individual only the week before and it had been separated from its companions, lying rather awkwardly on an island and looking ill. Now it had succumbed and was lying amidst some dense stands of rushes with two crows in attendance, each occasionally pecking at the apparently fresh carcase. One of the crows was a full black bird whilst the other was a typical hooded crow with the admixture of black and grey feathers. What concerned us was that last year some swans had been found dead in this part of Scotland from lead poisoning so we just hoped that this was not the start of another outbreak. The other birds on the loch, from a little grebe to tufted duck and a single Slavonian grebe to the overhead grey geese, did not compensate for our foreboding.

At the west end of the loch there are a few bushes forming a scrubby area, and more often then not there are reed buntings there and it is one of the few places in the Highlands where, these days, I can regularly see these attractive birds. On this visit I felt sure it was a family party as there was a male, a female and five what I took to be juveniles. They were just sitting on the top of a rose bush as if sunning themselves after a feed. When I was a warden of Castor Hanglands near Peterborough in the early 1970s, I would find the nests of reed buntings in quite marshy ground, and then a few years later the bird seemed to change its habitat. It started breeding in quite dry places which could have been the effect of so much drainage being undertaken. It is also interesting that the historical decline of this bird is mirrored by a similar decline in numbers of linnets and tree sparrows. Surely it cannot be a coincidence that all three feed on small grasses and herb seeds, especially farmland weeds. For most of the Highlands, breeding reed buntings are classed as 'scarce or local', although in some areas such as the Uists and parts of Caithness it used to be widespread.

As we were about to leave the loch a bird suddenly called as it came flying in, and they were the unmistakable notes of a green-shank and soon two of these delightful waders were feeding at the water's edge. I wondered where they might have come from and whether they might overwinter as a few do in other parts of the Highlands, such as perhaps the most regular wintering area for them at the Mound Alderwoods near Golspie on the east coast.

The colours of the group of eight wild goats that included two kids was typical of those found in the tribe that frequent the strath near the River Findhorn. Both the kids of the year were white and may well have been twins by the way they were behaving. The shape of the heads of the kids indicated that one was likely to be a billy and the other a nanny. An old nanny was of the silvery grey type with another younger beast black and white, another black all over and the rest all white. The group was feeding amidst some overgrazed juniper and gorse and with the wind in my favour I was within 20 yds (18 m) of them before they realised I was there. The immediate reaction was that they moved closer together but then instead of moving off each goat seemed unaware of what to do and their displacement reactions varied considerably.

The older nanny started nibbling her front legs whilst two younger nannies started butting each other's heads. Another nanny nibbled the end shoots of a juniper bush whilst the two kids nibbled each other on the back as if they were grooming each other. I advanced slowly and simply whistled which seemed to fascinate them whilst I took photographs of individuals and groups – all on black and white film. Then, as if by a signal between them, they turned their backs as one and slowly walked away to the base of a small cliff but still only 30 yds (27 m) away from me and I left them peacefully grazing.

It was not really a question of actually stalking them with my camera as I stood upright all the time. Whilst I was concentrating on the viewfinder I kept seeing slight movements nearer the ground out of the corner of my eyes as at least three mountain hares crept away under the low gorse and juniper. They were still in their brownish-grey autumn coats and using the low cover to hide from the local pair of golden eagles.

When the reintroduction programme of the sea eagle was under way I was, for a few days one year, responsible for feeding the young birds in their cages on the island of Rhum (now renamed Rum which is the original spelling). I well remember the sense of foreboding every time I went to feed them in case anything had happened to the birds since my previous visit. It was therefore with great interest two years ago that I paid a brief visit in the Highlands to the cages where the reintroduced red kites were being fed, as there was a fundamental difference in approach. The sea eagles had seen at least one person every day but with the red kites the cages were so positioned that they did not see anyone, even the people who fed them. I have seen the occasional reintroduced red kites in the 'wild' in the Highlands and whatever one thinks of such programmes and whether the birds are truly wild they are very attractive. A telephone call from a reader last week informed me that she had seen two buzzards and five red kites on fence posts on the same length of fence.

It is not often that we go to see a specific bird but the following day we went to the area where the five kites had been seen. As it happened we only located one red kite but it looked magnificent as it flapped across the narrow road in front of us looking rather like an elegant buzzard. The flight looked effortless as it circled over a grassy knoll where three Highland ponies were grazing and after a while I managed to get the telescope on the bird. The red feathers are best described as rufous and they contrast against the dark outer parts of the wing and the pale V-shaped feathers on the upper parts of the wings. The pale head feathers were conspicuous and in flight the red forked tail was obviously being used as a rudder to produce some effortless twisting and turning as the bird looked for food. As one bird book on British birds states 'Similar Species: none'.

Some days in the Highlands can be barren as far as wildlife is concerned but occasionally everything goes just right and such was the case in mid October when I went to a strath just south of Inverness. The first highlight was the sight of two golden eagles flying along a high ridge and the juvenile bird suddenly turned upside down and for a few seconds it touched the adult's talons with its own. Then further along the strath I sat in front of a steep hillside where there was a mosaic of scree and short juniper bushes between which a sparrow-hawk was hunting by dashing round bushes in the hope of finding an unwary small bird. Above this, at around the 1000 ft (305 m) contour, the snow began and further up it formed a blanket of white. On the snow line there was a red deer stag holding a harem of hinds and their calves and occasionally his head would go back, antlers lying along his back, and the ensuing roar echoed along the hillside where at opposite ends two stags roared back.

I could hear a buzzard 'mewing' behind me whilst I watched five ravens playing in the updraught of wind next to a cliff that supported a few aspens. The ravens' acrobatics included a sudden vertical dive with wings closed as if trying to imitate a peregrine. Two mountain hares were scampering along the lower slope with one of them still in the autumn coat and the other rapidly changing into the white winter one. But my attention was drawn to three wild goats amidst some rocks and junipers. The silvery kid was quietly grazing but the nanny was busy trying to refuse the attentions of the young billy. The nanny had wisely half backed into a crevice and the billy was so annoyed it kept stamping its front feet and making a wickering call. The nanny won the contest and the billy went off to graze and the kid went to the nanny and nuzzled up as if after milk. I sat in the sunshine which was making the bronze and yellow birch leaves glow where the coal tits and goldcrests were seeking food.

On the Western Isles of Lewis and Harris very few people now keep any poultry because of increased predation by mink. Mink were originally introduced to Britain from North America in the late 1920s and kept on fur farms for their valuable pelts. Frequent escapes have meant that many parts of Britain have now been colonised and their success on Lewis and Harris has partly been because they have no competitors such as fox and pine marten. A large-scale mink trapping programme has now been started on the islands to try and control the population, not only with poultry in mind but also ground-nesting birds. One aim of the trapping programme is to stop the mink spreading to the more southerly islands – the Uists – where mink would have a devastating affect on the internationally important colonies of ground-nesting birds – especially waders – on the machair.

Nearer home the main problem these days with keeping poultry is predation by the increasing numbers of pine martens. In two villages only a few miles from our house nobody keeps poultry any more and our nearest neighbour half a mile away has now given up when the last of her birds were taken last month. So far we have not lost any of our hens, ducks and geese although it seems inevitable that our turn will come. The strath we live in has a wide variety of habitats suitable for pine martens and foxes with plenty of woodland for them to hunt and block scree for the pine martens to rear their young. At the last fall of snow I checked the garden and paddock for tracks and a pine marten had clambered all over the geese and duck hutches. Intriguingly, and possibly just as threatening, a badger had also been to the hutches having approached right up to the door of the geese hutch and the hutch where the hens roost. Pine martens have the unfortunate reputation of killing a large number of birds on one visit and are often condemned for this behaviour.

Some years ago I was standing at the edge of some birch woodland and had that strange feeling that I was being watched although I could see nothing. I stared intently into the dense thicket of trees for some time and then I saw a slight movement and looked through the binoculars. It was a pair of great tits less than 20 yds (18 m) away and they were busy feeding on some small branches. However the binoculars revealed that the great tits were not on branches but looking for insects on the antlers of a sika deer stag. The incident was unusual in itself as the camouflage was extraordinary for such a large animal so close, as all I could see of the deer were small parts of both antlers, half an ear and a muzzle.

However what the incident did indicate was the enormous problem now facing conservationists in Scotland over the hybridisation between the native red deer and the introduced sika deer. In the 1980s some experts were saying that the hybridisation could eventually mean the end of pure red deer in Scotland with these only being found on islands such as the Western Isles. Then the threat seemed to die down but now more hybrids are being seen and action must be taken; one measure is to try and stop any more sika colonising fresh ground. The incident over the great tits and the camouflage highlights the enormity of this task as most people agree that the secretive habits of the sika deer make them by far the most difficult deer in Scotland to cull. They frequent woodland even more than the native roe deer do and they rarely go on to open ground in daylight, although they will do this if no culling has taking place for some time. Sika deer were originally introduced into Scotland for sporting purposes or into deer parks where they frequently escaped or were let out, sometimes deliberately. One of the most frightening sounds to hear if you do not know what it is or it is unexpected is the call note of the sika stag, which is a piercing whistle.

Over the years my contacts with the Cluanie Deer Park Farm near Inverness have varied such as my advice on what to do with a pine marten they had 'found' in one of the hutches. Did I have any Indian runner duck's eggs for their incubator where young visitors could see eggs hatching and did I have a white silkie cockerel they could put to their silkie hens? It therefore came as a surprise recently when the owners sent me a long list of livestock and equipment for sale as they were reluctantly giving up the farm. Some of the livestock I would have really liked, such as one of the longhorn cattle, but space is the problem. A few Soay sheep would also have been welcome but I have my doubts about the so-called Boreray sheep which they class as a rare breed. I am not sure how the latter can be classed as a rare breed when it is reputed to have been created in the late nineteenth century when one of the old Hebridean sheep was crossed with an early type of Scottish Blackface. Some of the feral goats would also have been welcome but the paddock fence would not contain them and it is too wet.

So my interest was much more modest as I was after the two white Embden geese and, yes, I did remember to check they were both in fact geese and not ganders.The reason for this interest was the sex imbalance with the 12 geese already in the paddock as for some time one gander had been spending each night on his own in one of the three goose sheds and I was not happy about this as the gander was obviously lonely. The price for the two geese was agreed over the telephone and I promised to go through that weekend to look at hutches. It seemed rather sad looking round the once busy farm, although most of the stock for sale would not be going for two weeks. I ordered one goose shed, three hen houses – I never have enough – and four metal drinkers and admired the two white geese. The geese were picked up two weeks later and brought safely home.

The passing of a dear friend reminded me of the times we had spent watching wildlife together mainly on Inverpolly National Nature Reserve where at various times we were both wardens working for the Nature Conservancy Council. Bill Henderson was one of the 'old style' naturalists who knew a great deal about a wide variety of subjects but also had the ability suddenly to take an interest in an entirely new subject which in later years he did with dragonflies. His knowledge of wildlife was backed by practical expertise such as with boat handling, woodland management and deer management and he had that rare ability to pass on his expertise and enthusiasm to new staff, young or old. I recall sitting on top of Cul Mor at nearly 3000 ft (914 m) with Bill talking about 'his' reserve with typical enthusiasm and pointing out the gradual spread of woodland by enclosing areas against stock and deer. A boat trip round the marine islands was memorable with Bill counting the arctic and common terns in their breeding colonies which seemed to change islands in some years.

But it was not always on Inverpolly that we shared wildlife as there was the survey of the chequered skipper butterfly near Fort William. I still have the recording forms that Bill – despite his dislike of paperwork – had filled in accurately and meticulously. In the evenings we went out recording moths that had been attracted to 'sugar' that we had previously painted on trees. On another occasion we sat having lunch in an old Caledonian pine forest near Ullapool where we had been collecting pine cones for seed. We listened to the whistles of sika deer stags and discussed the effect of deer, sheep and overburning on woodland. The last time we had been together we stood outside the Visitor Centre at Knockan Cliff – a centre which owes its undoubted success to Bill's expertise and enthusiasm. We shared a love of the hills and that is where I will remember him.

The signs at the end of the drive to the Conference Centre at Battleby simply said 'Badger Workshop' and I had a vision of a line of badgers carrying hand tools striding purposefully towards the big house. The incident brought the only smile of the day as fellow badger enthusiasts gathered to discuss the problems that currently face badgers in Scotland. It was a sad story, unfortunately, as representatives from many organisations discussed individual incidents and trends that are worrying. We are spoilt in the Highlands in that although badgers do have problems with illegal and legal snares and many road casualties we do not have the same level of persecution that badgers are experiencing further south. One representative in the room told of 140 illegal snares he has removed on a number of estates in the last 18 months. In the Central Belt a survey had revealed that 58% of badger setts had been 'interfered' with in one way or another.

Badger baiting with dogs still takes place and is more widespread than was thought as more and more people take up the cause of the badger and more of the baiters are found. Badger baiting must be the wickedest thing we do to animals when you bear in mind that the animal is so strong it has to be injured in some way such as a broken leg or broken jaw to give any of the dogs a chance. I was reminded of the poet/naturalist John Clare's description of how a baited badger dies as first of all each individual dog is beaten off. Then all the dogs at once are set on the badger and Clare's last two lines from the poem *Badger* written in 1836 are:

Till kicked and torn and beaten out he lies

And leaves his hold and cackles, groans, and dies

I drove back in the rain somewhat depressed at what I had heard but at the same time slightly heartened by the positive interest in this fascinating animal. As I passed the nearest badger sett to home I smiled once again, as the badgers would have a good night in the rain because there would be plenty of worms around for them to eat – their favourite food.

Pine Tree

To stand in old Caledonian pine forest is awesome for a number of reasons but perhaps the main one is that this is now the nearest you can get to seeing what the old Wildwood of Britain would have been like. At Amat the forest is one of the most northerly remnants of old Caledonian pine forest in the Highlands as it is a few miles inland from the Dornoch Firth on the east coast. Even on a rainy day the autumn colours of the birches and rowans contrasted with the old pine trees that towered over them and attracted crossbills which were calling. The river, called the Water of Glencalvie, was picturesque with the flaming colours of rowan and birch flanking its banks whilst several salmon were leaping as they passed through shallow water running over rounded stones. Sika deer are common in the area, having escaped from a former large deer park in Sutherland and the whistle of the stag at this time of year is very penetrating and rather frightening when heard for the first time. This is because you rarely see the stag as it calls from dense undergrowth. Just to the west of the forest I visited the small church at Croick and the only time I have been so moved by a church was the first time I went into the church on St Kilda many years ago.

In 1845 Croick church had been the sanctuary for people having been cleared from the land in the area and they had sheltered under canvas outside the walls. Their names are etched in the glass of the windows of the church although it is not quite clear who actually put the names there. The fate of these people was mixed, with some moving into other areas nearby whilst some went to the coast and others – like so many from the infamous clearances – went abroad. There is a feeling about the church and the land that cannot be explained: perhaps it was the futility of their defiance epitomised by the writing on the glass. Perhaps their souls are now resting there.

Prior to being interviewed for BBC radio about gorse I mentioned the two famous quotes about the flowering of this shrub, namely, 'while gorse is in flower Britain will never be conquered', and, 'when the gorse is out of bloom, kissing is out of fashion'. I then made the mistake of saying that patriots and lovers need not worry because some blossoms of gorse can be found all the year round. I was then challenged to find some so we set out for the moorland and heathland areas just south of Inverness where there are hundreds of acres of gorse. After an hour of searching – mainly from the road – it was somewhat embarrassing that I could not find a single blossom!

The final interview took place on the Drummossie Moor where each spring the stonechats use this evergreen shrub as their nesting sites along with linnets and, nearer the adjoining woodland, long tailed tits. But the interview was more about people and gorse and where we stood someone had obviously used it as a stockproof hedge but unusually the line of gorse was on either side of a burn, perhaps because it had a very muddy bottom and the gorse was being used to keep stock away. I then mentioned that the young shoots were readily browsed by sheep and the pyramidal shapes of the individual shrubs were all round us looking like hand-cut topiary. In the old days the old parts of the gorse were used as fodder but they had to be crushed in one way or another and at one time special whin bruisers or whin mills were used. The mills either used a roller or a wheel to crush the chopped gorse as it was fed into a channel. Gorse has also been used medicinally for man and animals and a medicine made from the blossoms was supposed to cure jaundice and stones in the kidney. In contrast gorse wine made from the blossoms is still very popular and they have also been used to flavour whisky. The blossoms and bark have been used as a dye and still provide a yellow colour used in the making of tartan cloth.

The barter system still survives in the Highlands as I have found out again this summer. It all started when someone called at the house and asked if I had any silkies to spare – he was looking for a replacement cock as his had been predated and he still had three silkie hens. Telephone numbers were exchanged but when looking at what silkies were available I suddenly realised that the person concerned would be passing the house again about 20 minutes later.

A large cardboard box and baler twine soon contained the necessary bird and I stopped the car in question. I was told that the person had no money with him but I said as the bird was free to a good home it did not matter. A few days later a $6^1/_2$ lb (3 kg) salmon arrived on the doorstep! A few weeks later the same person was looking for some khaki campbell ducks and again I refused any money for them and a few days later two pieces of venison arrived on the doorstep, one from a sika deer and the other from a roe deer.

Last week I fetched some maran and pekin hens from the next door neighbour half a mile away and these will be willingly looked after whilst the owners are away on holiday as it is these neighbours who always sort out any problems over the private water supply. Last time this involved cleaning out the tanks because we had comments about the purity of the water from the local authority who by law had to make a chemical check on the water supply. There had been talk of an expensive filter and other equipment but an independent analysis indicated it might only be sludge in the bottom of the tanks. The tanks had been cleaned out and the water supply re-tested and it proved acceptable so there was no legal obligation to fit a filter although it was advisable. A filter has not been fitted as I like having a bath in brown peaty water after stormy weather.

When we moved into this strath over eight years ago there were more breeding birds on the grassland and rough grazing. Common snipe 'drummed' and lapwings fluttered like large butterflies but the birds I miss the most are the skylarks. Nationally the latest figures indicate that in the last 20 years the numbers are down 60%. So it was fitting and timely that an anthology on the skylark, *An Exaltation of Skylarks* by Stewart Beer, should land on my desk. It is the most thought-provoking book I have read for some years and, remarkably, covers poems and prose over 23 centuries! Some of the authors have only one contribution included, such as Henry Williamson, but how apt the line: 'I am at one with the sunlight, and the lark is my brother.'. Others such as William Wordsworth had three poems and it was with bated breath that I looked up my favourite poet – John Clare – only to find that his five poems were the largest contribution of any in the book. His poem *The Skylark Leaving her Nest* was written in the 1830s and some of the lines epitomise my own feeling about skylarks:

> Right happy bird so full of mirth
> Mounting and mounting still more high
> To meet morns sunshine in the sky
> Ere yet it smiles on earth.

But there are other authors such as Thomas Hardy, Richard Jefferies and John Keats and they form, in the words of Stewart Beer, a 'tribute to this inimitable bird'. Hail to thee, blithe spirit. But the book is much more than a tribute as it throws down a challenge to all of us as to what we are going to do about the bird's possible extinction if the decline continues. Little wonder then that the shorthand name of the British Trust for Ornithology's Farmland Birds Appeal is SOS (Save our Skylarks). Publishers are SMH Books, Pear Tree Cottage, Watersfield, Pulborough, West Sussex.

Even from the outside the Tugnet ice house is impressive, particularly as it is standing where the wide estuary of the River Spey meets the Moray Firth. The ice house is reputed to be the largest one to have survived and it now contains a summer exhibition on the history of salmon catching in the area. The building is dated 1830 and measures 62 by 56 ft (19 by 17 m) and it can be seen from a distance looking like three barrel-vaulted structures set in sloping ground.

The trade must have been very important to the economy of this coastline as records from 1842 indicate that the London market took 600 boxes of salmon packed in ice, each weighing 34 lbs (15.4 kg) and worth £5. As if epitomising the role of salmon in the area 55 yds (50 m) away in the rapidly ebbing tide there were several grey seals and two mature bulls were each tackling a large salmon. Birds such as goldeneye and red-breasted merganser were floating out on the water whilst redshank and turnstone flew over. There were waders everywhere including common snipe that were calling as if alarmed. The reason was a male hen harrier flying low over the reed beds, hunting. Most of the ones I see in the Highlands are either immature, or adult females, and both are mainly brown so it was exciting to see the pale grey plumage of an adult male.

I walked along some of the raised mounds of pebbles which separated the sea from the estuary and there, tucked on the landward side of one ridge and protected from the cold wind, was a party of about a hundred dunlin that from the distance looked like grey foam scattered on the pebbles. I photographed the old boats outside the ice house, they were called salmon cobles and with six oars were larger than conventional boats. The last two frames were used up on the impressive sculpture standing on a plinth. It was of a flying osprey with – as one would have expected – a salmon in its talons.

The red deer stag was roaring from across the strath but he was still difficult to find on the high slopes above the River Findhorn. Then, through the telescope, he came into view and I could actually see his mouth open although it took the sound a few seconds to reach me. His harem was close by, consisting of 17 hinds and calves but they were quietly grazing and ignoring the belligerent stag. Two other stags were sounding out their challenge from different parts of the strath and it was likely that this would be as far as it would go – vocal protests in the rut. Books may well talk of stags fighting to the death but most so called battles are settled by roaring at each other or eyeing each other up at closer quarters, although just occasionally fights will take place. Edwin Landseer's *Monarch of the Glen* was a flight of fancy as in the red deer world a matriarchy exists.

Then above the red deer nine ravens suddenly appeared and they were playing in the wind, rising and tumbling down as if learning to fly for the first time. One raven landed and the others circled as if concerned although I could see no reason for this behaviour. Another raven strayed too far along a steep cliff face where a rowan was red with autumn colouring and suddenly, as if from nowhere, it was chased off by a peregrine falcon and made to return to the other ravens. The saying I know about ravens only goes up to three so I wonder what nine would mean? 'To see one raven is lucky tis true, But it's certain misfortune to light upon two, And meeting with three is the devil.' Ravens have always featured strongly in myth and folklore and have always been credited with the powers of prediction. When Macaulay visited St Kilda in the eighteenth century he wrote that of all the birds the raven was believed by the St Kildans to be 'the most prophetical'. My favourite nest is in a remote corrie on the Sutherland border and below the nest there is a large colony of purple saxifrage (which is in flower when the ravens are nesting).

In wildlife terms it is easy to make mistakes and the recent publication of a book on golden eagles reminded me of such an event on a hill not too far from Inverness. I was taking part in a selective survey of eagle territories and it was a long but satisfying walk into the cliff face. Red deer – both hinds and stags – seemed everywhere, indicating that the problem of over-population in some parts of the Highlands has not gone away. I soon found the first eyrie and I wrote down in my notebook that the nest had not been lined so the eagles had not nested that particular year. I decided to walk up round the cliff and it was then that I found another suitable-looking site by – needless to say – a rowan tree. There on a wide ledge was another eyrie but this time it had been lined and even a cup for eggs had been formed but there was no sign of any eggs, or for that matter any adult eagles. Out came the notebook in which I wrote that the eagles had formed a complete nest including the egg cup but for some reason had not laid and the territory was deserted.

I then scrambled up to the top of the cliff where I sat on a flat area covered with quite tall heather. I made a few more notes but then my concentration was broken by a call note and it was apparent it was from a nestling and my first thought was a golden eagle chick. Then I dismissed the idea, as an empty golden eagle nest was just below me and the sound seemed very close. I searched everywhere and then suddenly there in the heather on flat ground was a nest scrape with a golden eagle chick. I made a mental note to write down later that this was a hastily constructed nest as the eagle had been disturbed at the other nest below and this chick was probably from a second clutch. I stepped backwards from the nest and tripped over something in the heather and there were the remains of a photographer's hide from the year before. As far as the three eyries were concerned I had made mistakes on all of them.

The doors to the hall in this east coast town were late in opening and it was tantalising waiting as we could hear ducks quacking from inside. Then a small group of us shuffled through the narrow doorway and we were into the tenth Annual Show of the Sutherland Poultry Club. The first bird I saw was a white Indian runner duck that was being transferred to a taller cage as its neck was too long. The bird instantly amused me as they look so comical which is one of the reasons I have ten white ones and five black. The first row of cages held the bantams, both light breed and heavy breed classes. I particularly like the light Sussex although in general I am not very keen on such small birds. Then to 'proper' hens as I call them such as the australorps which looked enormous although I doubt they were as big as mine, especially the cockerel, or males as the catalogue called them. The Rhode Island reds were as big as the ones my father used to breed many years ago and I remember his used to kill brown rats. I did have some Rhode Island reds once but against someones advice I let a bantam cockerel in with the cockerel and the bantam killed it within a few minutes before I realised what was happening.

The duck section at the show was the noisiest, with one duck quacking the whole time I was in the hall. There were some very impressive birds on show with plenty of rosettes on cages and in the corner was a table weighed down with cups, medals and plaques waiting for the award ceremony in the afternoon. I was told the judges took from 9.30 that morning until after 1 o'clock and I could well believe this as choosing the winners must have taken some heart searching. One breed of duck impressed me so much I am thinking about getting some for next summer. These were cayuga ducks and they were large and almost black and the drake in particular was very regal looking.